52 Reasons for Hope

Finding Inspiration in
Times of Trouble

Lisa —

it's been a pleasure
watching your blossoming

Keep hoping

52 Reasons for Hope

Finding Inspiration in Times of Trouble

by

Cathy Krizik

newmorning
MEDIA

Copyright © 2019 Cathy Krizik
All rights reserved.

No part of this publication may be reproduced, distributed, or transmitted in any form or by any means, including photocopying, recording, or other electronic or mechanical methods, without the prior written permission of the publisher, except in the case of brief quotations embodied in critical reviews and certain other noncommercial uses permitted by copyright law.

For permission requests, email the author, at:
permission@cathykrizik.com

Santa Cruz, CA
www.newmorningmedia.com
(831)332-5859

Cover, photography and book design by Cathy Krizik

Printed in the United States of America

In the midst of winter,
I found there was,
within me,
an invincible summer.

—ALBERT CAMUS

Table of Contents

Reflections

Appendix

Acknowledgments

IMAGINE A WRITER WRITING AND you'll invariably envision them alone. Maybe they're in an attic office, hunched over a typewriter, caught in the beam of a lamp. In the scene you might find piles of paper, a cup of coffee, a window through which to gaze, maybe even a cat curled on a dusty braided rug. But no people. Even writers who prefer writing in crowded cafes will likely be wearing earbuds, lost in their own thoughts because writing happens behind the gates of the mind. Writers write alone.

Yet we write *for* people, *about* people, *to* people. We write *around* people. We write *from* people because we write about life and life is, at heart, a communal experience.

For the last five years I've slipped out of bed before dawn so I could write alone. But as I tiptoed down the hall, a constellation of people came with me. As I slipped into my favorite chair and opened my laptop, a legion of friends, relatives, colleagues, therapists, teachers, even strangers gathered around me, whispering, cajoling, cheering me on when my faith floundered. Every interaction I've ever had is, in some small way, woven into every sentence in this book. My third grade teacher, the neighbor lady with the maps, that fight with the gas station attendant in Brooklyn in 1981 all coalesce to make me who I am. Part of me wants to fill pages with their names and stories. As I put the final touches on this book, they all feel important. But I'll control myself and focus instead on the voices—and deeds—that whispered the loudest.

To my Thursday night and "Writing Journey" tribe.
There is not a sentence, not a comma or deleted adverb, that doesn't bear your fingerprints. Your marginalia question marks, underlines, and gently offered feedback made me a better writer. Thank you Jennifer Astone, Nancy Brown, Susan Burrowes, Sheila Coonerty, Vanya Erickson, Melinda Iuster, Magali Morales, Larae Ross, Molly Segale, Renee Winter, Debby Bates, Paldrom Collins, Gavriella Delgado, Nancy Guither, Becky Hall, Marie Hanson, Christine Holmstrom, Olivia Lehrman, Claire Lovell, Danilyn Rutherford, Laurie Simpkinson, Robin Somers, Linda Statzer, and every other writer with whom I've shared a circle. Your unerring support has enriched my life immeasurably.

To my writing teachers, Laura Davis and Susan Brown.
You taught me how to tell stories. You taught me that putting words on a page is only the beginning—that real writers

edit, then edit some more. While your honesty wasn't always easy to hear, it was always—always—appreciated. Your commitment to truth-telling on the page and your unrelenting high standards spurred me to be my best. If this book is any good, it's largely due to you.

To my beta readers. Cath Byrne, Kaylie Duggan, Kawami Evans, Beth Love, Veronica McGlynn, Magali Morales and Siobhan Nash. Your willingness, insights and generosity humble me. You are woven into every page.

To Rev. Deborah L. Johnson. Underneath the writing itself is the message and that's all you. The beating heart of this book is a set of spiritual principles—a framework, a philosophy, a way of understanding the world—that I learned at your feet. Thank you for introducing me to a God I could befriend. My life is better thanks to you.

To my brother Kent. You have witnessed my every step and stumble. You alone know what happened inside those walls and I'm grateful you have been willing to revisit them with me. It's comforting to know I needn't carry the memories alone. Thank you for your steadfast, loving presence all these years.

To my parents and their parents and their parents before them. I carry your legacy proudly—and mindfully. I'm the beneficiary of a family that has brightened the world but also cast shadows. I hope I have put the privilege and gifts I've been given to good use.

And lastly, to my Judit. Thank you for our life. For your unwavering support of my creative impulses. For modeling perseverance. For reading, editing, listening and nudging me to the truth only you knew I was avoiding. For loving me in spite of the thousands of hours I spent away from us as I disappeared into this book. You are my ballast, my warrior, my love.

Introduction

THIS IS A BOOK ABOUT hope and hope is, fundamentally, about the future. It's about daring to envision a world that shines a little brighter, feels a little kinder. To hope is to believe in our capacity to create a better tomorrow.

Yet we live in today and, let's face it, today is a bit of a mess.

Regardless of your politics, what God you worship (if any), the tribes you claim, or how many zeros you have in your bank account, I think we can agree that society is faltering. Institutions are crumbling; technology is on a bender; injustice persists; and, if hurricanes, fires and floods are any indication, Mother Nature isn't happy. Add the tyranny of everyday life to the brew of global troubles and you'd be excused for feeling deluged. Life—and, yes, optimism—can be hard, especially if you're paying attention.

How do we manage the dissonance?

Mostly, we react. We scream at the TV. We download mindfulness apps and barely give them a minute. We fret and flail and pop Ativan. We go numb, eat too much, shop too much and, my personal favorite, binge-watch *Downton Abbey*. Avoidance, in all its permutations, is an excellent coping mechanism. It works to quiet the noise and dull the senses—that is, until we reflexively reach for our smart phone and everything we'd been trying to avoid comes flooding back: Mom has cancer, Washington is broken, sea levels are rising, and a gunman just leaned out of a hotel window and unleashed his AR-15 on a crowd of concert-goers in Las Vegas.

Hope can be hard to muster in a world gone mad. In spite of all our efforts to the contrary, and as hard as it is to accept, we are powerless over most of what happens in life. Circumstances blow in from the four directions without our permission yet we maintain control over one wild and crafty thing, a tool that is always at the ready—our mind.

Obstacles and struggles arrive at our doorstep every day. I once came home from work to discover that my hot water heater had burst, releasing a river into my living room where the carpet drank the flood like a thirsty man in the desert. My emotions rolled from shock to fury to exasperation as my socks went sloppy cold. But then I noticed the sun streaming through the rhododendron bush outside my front window. The light dappling my bookshelves was lovely and utterly unconcerned with my failed water heater. I took a deep breath, then another, and in that sliver of an opening my mind went quiet and I had one of those fulcrum moments when a simple insight changes everything. I came to understand that I could choose what to think, choose how to respond. I had the capacity to decide how to react. Calm felt better than frantic. So I chose calm.

Our mind is ours, therefore, ours to command. If we're conscious, we get to choose how we experience the hardships—and good fortune—we're handed.

I'm not naive. I know it's not easy. Our minds are ruthless creatures of habit. I understand that stepping off familiar, long-traveled paths requires discipline. But I also know it's possible—even imperative—if we want to live a fulfilling life in a peaceful, loving universe.

We live the life we think about so why not think about the life we want most deeply? Why not envision, believe in, imagine—hope for—a world that works for everyone?

Why not, indeed? That's why I wrote 52 Reasons for Hope.

What are these words and how can they help?

Unlike the chair I sit on and the mug of Earl Grey by my side, the words in this book are formless. They are concepts, qualities that can't be examined under a microscope or held in our hands. They can't be heard, smelled or tasted. They are, in and of themselves, invisible—as immaterial as breath, as seemingly impermanent as a dream. Yet they are the grandest power in the universe.

We think of joy, clarity and wisdom as transient feelings or abstract ideas we get to enjoy only when circumstances and conditions line up in our favor. We think of whole-ness, creativity, vulnerability—and all the fifty-two qual-ities—as more mercurial and less dependable than, say, a rock. But that's not true. The chair I sit on may be solid. It's material existence is indisputable. But one day it will turn to dust. Even the concrete under my feet can be pulverized back into the sand it once was.

People, places and things are ephemeral but these prin-ciples are not. Love is always available. Hope is always an option. Compassion is always an alternative. Oneness is always a solution. For everyone. The only thing transient and ephemeral about these qualities is whether we choose to embody them or not.

THE CHALLENGES WE FACE are deep enough to swallow a bus. Political and economic interests are entrenched. Modern life is bedlam. The human heart is fragile. Yet, inside each of us, is a vault of riches—infinite and eternal—from which to draw. Past the madness and through the thorny brambles is a reservoir of sweet, still waters—the antidote to all that ails us.

And, the best part? The gifts are ours for the asking. We don't have to earn them. We needn't pass a test or do good deeds to deserve them. They are ours simply for being human—a bounty handed out at birth.

52 Reasons for Hope is an invitation to harness the power of that magic to reshape our day, thrive in our lives and, maybe—if we're willing—begin to heal the world's wounds.

How to use this book

There is a long tradition of reading inspirational books to set one's mind on a more affirming, more heart-centered path. My hope is that this book follows in that tradition—motivating, enlivening, arousing in you new ways of relating to the world's wonders and challenges.

Read one reflection a day, one a week or whenever you notice your mind bumbling down a bumpy, unhelpful road. Read them in order or fan the pages until the book parts of its own accord. The choice is yours.

Use each reflection as a subject of meditation. Use them as affirmations, prayers, topics for dinner table conversations, prompts for a writing practice. Or, do what I do. Pick a word, carry it with you through the day, look through its lens and watch it bloom in surprising, illuminating ways. But, take heed. As Rumi said, "What you seek is seeking you." Thoughts are powerful. They multiply. Ask for faith and your faith may be tested. Pray for patience and you may be handed ample opportunities to practice patience. Hope for peace in the world and all the reasons it seems impossible may rise up to meet you.

The impact of these qualities will be measured by your willingness to be conscious and embody them. Persistence and discipline are required. After all, kindness is only a word until it is put into action. Plant the seed, tend your garden and watch it blossom. My hope is that you do more that read these passages. My hope is that you live them. ~

Reflections

Vision

Imagining the future we want to inhabit

I CAN SEE FURTHER WITH my eyes closed. We all can. I can see the house of my future, the one on a hillside with a wide wooden deck overlooking a verdant forest where deer forage and red-tailed hawks nest. I can see myself at eighty, my body as strong as a sequoia, my mind as supple as its finest branches. The images may be formless, nothing more than shimmering dreams whipped up by my imagination, yet they have life. Power. Influence. Consequence. They come with feelings that spark and crackle, motivating us into action.

The present world—the one we see before us—isn't pretty. The ugliness arrives everyday. Violence. Greed. Governments plagued by division and discord. It's easy to feel trapped. Hopeless. The wall is too high to climb, too barbed to overcome. Yet we set up camp at its base and spend our days cowering in its cold shadow.

We needn't. In the face of a wall why not grab a shovel and start digging...build a ladder...learn to rock climb?

Like pioneers and freedom seekers everywhere, the impediments are never as big as the rewards that lie beyond them.

The world needs our dreaming. It deserves our best thinking, ideas, hopes. The troubles we face are real but the perception that they hold us captive is not. With vision we look into the future and dare to name the world we want. With vision imbued with faith we see beyond the horizon to a field waiting for sowers. With spade and seed, we plant a garden, watch it grow and invite all to come and taste the sweet fruit of our making.

—⚒—

The oak sleeps in the acorn,
the bird awaits in the egg,
and in the highest vision of the soul
a waking angel stirs.
Dreams are the seedling of realities.

—JAMES ALLEN

Power

The capacity to produce an effect

I F YOU SAW ME ON the street, you probably wouldn't think I was a lesbian. I wear lipstick, blow dry my hair and prefer linen to flannel. Most people assume I'm straight. But I'm not. Back in the 1980s, when holding hands in public was a risky, defiant act, I counted myself lucky. As long as I kept my hands in my pockets, I could wander through my queer life in relative safety. But as the AIDS epidemic raged and I grew up, a sense of obligation set in. Staying quiet began to hurt. So I began coming out. Consciously. In line at the supermarket, in the lunchroom with colleagues, around the pool at my mom's condo, I'd casually mention "my partner" and make sure to insert "she" for clarity.

It was a gentle act. No grandstanding, no flexing of muscles. Just a simple statement of fact offered with an easy shrug. Sharing a piece of my life with a taxi driver or bank teller or front desk clerk was seemingly insignificant but when my lone voice joined with others, we became a roaring chorus that changed the world. Gay marriage is now legal because, in part, millions of men and women took a deep breath, summoned their courage, and told a quiet truth. Power can be as soft as a whispered confession.

Normally we think of power as a force in someone else's hands, something wielded over us. It looms in the boss, the suit on Wall Street, the barrel of a cop's Glock. But power is exercised when the disenfranchised vote…when the meek find their voice…when we take the time to listen to another human being so they feel heard.

How we exert our influence is our choice. A 140-character tweet can lift the world to its promise or tear it down. We can brandish a club or offer a hand, laugh at a hateful joke or not. Power doesn't reside only in presidential palaces or country clubs or a judge's gavel. It lives in our every action—in daring to be who we are. Tell the truth, express yourself, offer a kind word to a stranger and watch the ripples encircle the earth.

—∞—

Power needn't be big and brash.
Even a faltering flame can vanquish
the darkness.

—CK

Beauty

A manifestation of life's artistry

BEAUTY RESIDES IN EVERY CORNER and plain. The leaves of an aspen, lemon yellow and taut, flicker in the Colorado wind. Mountains rise from the plains and shine on the surface of a still lake. Peregrine falcons, sparrows and starlings wing between city skyscrapers. At dawn and dusk, no matter the longitude or latitude, the sun performs an opera of color.

And sharing the planet with snow leopards and dancing northern lights are human beings—every one of us blazing with an inborn impulse to love. Mothers, fathers, sisters, brothers, friends, neighbors, citizens—each leavened with a yearning to nurture and care. Evidence abounds: the offer of a seat on a crowded bus; the bulging bags of condolence mail delivered to disaster survivors from faraway strangers; tears that swell and spill at a wedding, graduation, hospital bedside. All emanations of beauty in human form.

Beauty sometimes hurts but only because we believe it is fleeting. The spirit will always soar. The heart will always swell. Our mind may turn away but the lotus will always bloom, petals to the sky, a bequest for the eyes.

—⚭—

A thing of beauty is a joy for ever:
Its loveliness increases;
it will never pass into nothingness.
— JOHN KEATS

Courage

*Perseverance in the face of
danger and difficulty*

L OOK TO NELSON MANDELA, Harvey Milk, Cesar
Chavez. Look to the weekend hiker who decides to
tackle Half Dome without ropes; the environmen-
talist who chains herself to an old growth redwood in front
of loggers; the battered woman who finally scoops up her
kids and flees into the night. When darkness presses in
too tight, when all the easy cards have been played, when
our gifts chafe and scream to be fully expressed, there is
a reservoir of strength—bottomless and enduring—from
which to draw.

I used to think of myself as failing at courage. I won't
ride rollercoasters or jump out of airplanes or lay my life
on the line for a cause. As a rule, I'm adrenalin avoidant.
But preferring a calm cruise on the Caribbean to white
water rafting doesn't make me a coward. Sometimes just
being myself takes courage.

I was raised by atheists. We were devotees of the *New York*

Times—educated, rational people who thought spirituality was better left to airheads and suckers. To write a book that includes talk of the soul, consciousness and prayer is to commit family heresy. To dare to think my words worthy of your time e is to stand naked in the public square and hand out cameras. I can hear the snickers now, see the rolling eyes. The thought makes me wince and ache for the back of a deep, dank cave.

Yet, I proceed, thanks to courage—the animating force inside that pushes us past our fear to our most transcendent selves. Courage is the rocket fuel or the slow burn of smoldering embers that propels us to heed the inner call—to run into the burning building or sit quietly in the sun writing about divinity. To be courageous is to act on things that feel impossible when they are, in fact, imperative. To be courageous is to affirm the magnificence and power of the human spirit, regardless of the price.

—✺—

It takes courage to grow up and
become who you really are.

— E. E. CUMMINGS

8

Forgiveness

Choosing love in the face of misdeed

S OMETIMES, I LIE IN BED at night and seethe. Some insult, some injury has been committed against me, so I stare at the shadows on the ceiling and recall each infraction, catalogue each wrongdoing for later reference. Brick by brick, I construct a wall between me and the villain and stand firm, hardened for the fight.

But the fight never comes. I'm alone behind my barricade, my mind swirling in fury.

The human heart is tender and we struggle to keep it safe. Sometimes that means shuttering ourselves away; other times we lash out. But when we choose to forgive, we take a different path. We don't retreat or attack. We stand still in the tornado and make a choice to open our hearts wider than we ever thought possible.

In 2006, a man walked into a one-room Amish schoolhouse in Lancaster County, Pennsylvania, and shot ten girls before turning the gun on himself. His act was, by most standards, the definition of evil. Unforgivable. But before the sun had set the following day, the entire community had gathered to offer their forgiveness to the murderer and his family.

Forgiveness isn't easy. It's a process, a muscle that needs to be flexed, nourished, stretched. The deeper the wound, the longer it may take to heal. The pain becomes a faithful, familiar companion. I know this from experience.

For decades, I stirred a pot of resentment toward my mother. She was flawed and I wanted better. Through my twenties, thirties, and forties, her shortcomings simmered on my back burner. But when she called one day and, through tears, told me she couldn't bring herself to eat, I walked into a therapist's office and handed myself over. "My mother's health is failing. Help me to not hate her when she dies."

Week after week, we dissected my rancor and nursed my hurt feelings. Two years and a long and ragged road later, I sat at my mom's hospice bedside, holding her hand, stroking her cooling forehead, loving her wholeheartedly.

Forgiveness is a gift we give ourselves. To forgive is not to forget but to look through the circumstances to the soul beyond the story. We all miss the mark. To forgive is to acknowledge our fallibility, our frailty, the ease with which we all veer off the path. To find peace is to unburden ourselves of the bitterness and reach, instead, for the sweet reward of forgiveness.

—∞—

To forgive is to set a prisoner free
and discover the prisoner is you.

—Lewis B. Smedes

Stillness

An invitation to be with oneself

STANDING AT MY KITCHEN WINDOW, I watched a hummingbird hover in the air above a pot of succulents. Its iridescent green crown and black needle nose were rock still as its wings vibrated in a blur. Soon it cocked its head and flickered across the patio, drawn by the red stamen of a fuchsia bloom, then zipped over the fence. It was a bundle of industry, twisting and gyrating, flitting from thing to thing, idleness unthinkable.

That's how I live my life. Time exists to be filled. The thirty seconds it takes for hot water to arrive in my kitchen sink so I can wash the dishes is an eternity. So, as I wait, I set the kettle to boil, pull out a mug, grab a teabag, measure a teaspoon of sugar, retrieve the milk from the refrigerator, pour a glug and return to the sink to find the water only just heading towards tepid. Thirty seconds of doing nothing is inconceivable.

But then, there's meditation. My first attempt was, like a first kiss, too self-conscious to enjoy. As sandalwood incense tickled my nose, I sat crossed-legged in my college dorm room and lit a candle. Hands on knees, guru-style, I took long, deep breaths and stared into the flame which bobbed and weaved on the breeze of my exhale. My mind raced. My feet tingled. An intolerable itch screamed for attention. I endured the placidity for five minutes before jumping up to smoke a cigarette. It would take years of intermittent effort before I developed a meditation practice that allowed me anything close to stillness.

Today, I light the candle, curl up on my couch and ride the winds of my mind, observing its patterns and power. But when the stars deem it so, I am granted a glimpse of an empty expanse, a stage, an open pasture where the air is clean, the vista broad and there is nothing in me that needs fixing. In that stillness is a summoning, an invitation to a place where possibilities are limitless.

Stillness knows no judge. It holds no ill will, wants nothing in return. In stillness, there is no doing, no expectation, only being, and the Being I find there—me—is as miraculous as the hummingbirds in my garden.

—❧—

Within you, there is a stillness and a sanctuary to which you can retreat at any time and be yourself.

—HERMANN HESSE

Being

A state of existence

SIX MONTHS AFTER MY MOTHER died, in a fog of complicated grief, I was offered refuge at a dear friend's cabin in Canada. For a week, I sat on her worn wooden deck, resting my eyes on the glassy surface of Shoal Lake. We fished, gave one another foot massages and drank Sauvignon Blanc. But the moment carved most deeply in my memory is our drive west into the great expanse of the Manitoba prairie. On a single lane road, with nothing but sky from horizon to horizon and bales of hay to measure the miles, she pulled the car over. I got out and walked into the field. As a warm breeze swept across the green barley, I pulled my hands from my pockets and stood still. In that place, in the presence of my mother's absence, at the fulcrum between past and future, I felt myself alive. As savannah sparrows flew overhead, I felt the rush of my blood, the legacy of my ancestors, the blessing of grief and all the choices I'd made that brought me to that moment, in that patch of pasture.

This is who I am. This is me—being.

There are, in my mind, two worlds—the physical and spiritual. In the former, we do—we move our bodies through space. We work, cook dinner, hold hands with those we love. The spiritual world, by contrast, exists in the wilds of consciousness—an intangible, ethereal place where we feel, intuit, know without language or form.

Being is the act of straddling both worlds. Here we're aware of our circumstances and our divinity simultaneously. To be is to set judgment and expectation aside and take note of the moment. Being is where blessings rise from what remains. Where dragonflies flit, clouds cast shadows on the grain, a mother's love warms and I stand tall on Canadian soil, a grateful witness.

—⚊⚊—

I took a deep breath and listened
to the old brag of my heart.
I am, I am, I am.

—SYLVIA PLATH

Oneness

The state of inextricable connection

I N MEDITATION, WHEN MY THOUGHTS are stuck in the mire of my own circumstances, I have a routine. In my mind's eye, I travel the globe and imagine people in their lives. I conjure a woman washing down a side-walk in Paris....a doctor in Aleppo tending to an injured boy...a family trudging through the Sonoran Desert, heading north for the border. With each image, I step out of myself and the distance between us vanishes. My heart softens and I wonder whether these strangers know—in some quiet corner—that I'm thinking of them. I hope so.

Our senses tell us we are separate from one another, in-dependent and autonomous. We think we end at the edge of our skin—I'm here and you're there—but we don't. Like a tree is to the forest, like a wave is to the ocean, each of us is a piece of the whole. A single thread in a larger cloth. Singular in nature but indivisibly bound.

Oneness isn't easy. When I first heard my spiritual teacher use the phrase "we are all one," the cynic in me scoffed. All one? Yeah, sure. Tell that to the polluter, the homophobe, the suicide bomber, the hedge fund manager driving his Lamborghini. But now I understand. Whether we recognize it or not, we are like a string of dominos, dependent on one another in an infinite game of cause and effect. Physics tells us that every action sparks a reaction. The newspaper that doesn't get recycled ends up in a landfill that emits methane that warms the atmosphere that turns icebergs to seawater that floods island nations forcing families from their homes. In oneness we recognize that how we behave, talk, work, pray, vote has the capacity to change the world—for good or ill.

Like Rosa Parks on that Birmingham bus in 1955, we are far more powerful than we know. Drop a stone into a still pond and watch. The ripples expand outward and soon fade from view but we know that their effects are never-ending. This is the truth of oneness. In oneness, we hold the earth in our hands and care for one another as we would hope to be cared for ourselves because we are, in fact, all one.

—∞—

We all drink from one water
We all breathe from one air
We all rise from one ocean
And all live under one sky

—ANWAR FAZAL

Compassion

Deep sympathy for the misfortune of others

Y EARS AGO, I WAS ON vacation in Florida when a young man with dirty clothes, ragged beard and a wobbling limp approached me in a grocery store parking lot. I pulled my purse closer.

"I'm not asking for money," he said to my back. "I need food. My girlfriend's pregnant and we're living in that car."

I stopped and turned as he pointed to a rusty old Honda Civic with a crumpled bumper. Food? Pregnant? I looked into his face and saw a kind soul down on his luck, struggling to be a provider. Our eyes met. His fell to the asphalt and my cynicism evaporated. This was not a man used to asking for handouts. I reached out and gave his shoulder a gentle squeeze. "Come on. Let's see what we can do."

Together, we walked through the store and he picked out peanut butter, strawberry jelly and a family-sized loaf of whole wheat bread. I added a gallon jug of water. It was ninety degrees outside and he was living in a parking lot. Walking back to his car he shared his story—his mother's recent death, the eviction notice, the nursing degree deferred, the suicide attempt.

We all get scared and hungry. We all need a roof. We all endure loss. To bear witness to others' suffering is the gift of compassion. To be compassionate is to acknowledge and revere our common frailty—to hold hands with someone in the midst of their storm. Our capacity for compassion is evidence that, in spite of all our differences, we are more alike than we imagine.

—∞—

In separateness lies the world's
great misery, in compassion lies
the world's true strength.

— BUDDHA

Prayer

The art of moving consciousness

MY PARENTS WORSHIPPED AT THE altar of the *New York Times*. To us, God was nothing but wishful thinking. I was never baptized, never went to church, never said grace before dinner, never kneeled at the side of my bed, hands steepled like the kids on TV. I was certain praying was for fools until one day in college I found myself counting days on a calendar. Twenty-eight, twenty-nine, thirty...When I hit forty-four, the calender slipped from my hands and I spewed out my very first prayer. *Please God, oh please, if you're up there, I'll do anything, just please God, don't let me be pregnant.*

I cringed at my duplicity. The words felt foreign on my tongue. I was supposed to be an atheist yet there I was, at the first sign of trouble, surrendering my principles. But the pleading felt so good, it didn't matter that I was talking to a fantasy. I wasn't alone; there was someone to share my burden. A few days later, my cycle returned to normal and my worries were washed away, along with any memory of my lapse.

For years my prayers were reserved for moments of high drama but that changed when, on a whim, I accepted a friend's invitation to a spiritual community where I heard a message that, to my surprise, found a home in me. Under their roof, prayer was disentangled from religion and reconstituted into a tool I could wield to realign my mind. I learned that prayer didn't require submitting to an unseeable authority. Praying could also be a way to manage my thoughts—at least for the moment.

The mind can be a runaway train, barreling down well-travelled tracks through unhelpful territory. In prayer we get conscious. We put on the brakes, switch tracks and surrender the helm. But to whom? To what?

For those comfortable with God, these questions are easily answered. Believers know who's listening. But for the rest of us, the questions are confounding. For years, I agonized over who was listening to my appeals. Without a deity there was no one to hear my dormroom begging, no one to witness my pleas when cancer came calling, no one to accept my thanks for the countless blessings in my life. Without God, no one was listening

Except there *was* someone. Me. The one praying.

In prayer we hear, in our own words, what hurts, what we fear, what truly matters. In prayer, we come clean. We point our consciousness to the future and declare what we want most deeply: peace, courage, health, forgiveness, love. In prayer, we face the raw—sometimes beautiful, sometimes painful—truth and, in the airing, we create a gentler, more wholehearted life.

—∞—

The function of prayer is not to influence God, but rather to change the nature of the one who prays.

— Søren Kierkeggard

Magic

The bewitching power of the unexplained

A MAN AND WOMAN TOUCH, cavort between the sheets and nine months later a human being is born with a heart capable of beating thirty-seven million times a year—year after year—with barely a bobble.

Magic.

When an apple drops from a tree, it lands in the dirt with a soft thud. This we know. It's gravity. But how does gravity work? Why doesn't fruit float up through the branches and into the clouds? No one actually knows.

Magic.

Consider the mystery of love at first sight, the silent wonder of fireflies, the impulse to make art, the crisp perfume of lilac, the beautiful heartbreak of Yo-Yo Ma at the cello.

All magic.

There are, of course, experts who can explain away some of the mystery. Cardiologists know hearts. Physicists know equations that describe objects in space and time. When a magician saws a woman in half and—ta da!—she pops out of the box wholly alive, he understands the trick. But we don't. Our faces explode in big, satisfied smiles. Not understanding how it works is what makes it fun. That place of not knowing is where magic lives.

ABOVE ME RIGHT NOW ARE two mockingbirds in a phalanx of feather and wing, gyrating and butting chests as they squawk at one another like an old married couple. Thirty thousand feet above their flapping is an airplane full of people sleeping, reading and popping peanuts as they jet north at four hundred miles an hour. Past them, obscured in the luminous blue, are billions of stars, moons and planets including one "super-planet" in the constellation of Cancer that astronomers think is almost entirely made of—wait for it—diamond. Above us floats a diamond twice the size of earth.

If pondered over longer than a blink, the world we inhabit—and the life we live—is a mind-bending, ecstatic magic show. Is there a rational explanation for all the incomprehensible? Is there a master magician with all the answers? Is it God's sleight of hand? Or is it a wild game of dice with spectacular results? No one knows for sure and, dare I say, that's the best part. Like rabbits being pulled from hats, if we understood how it worked, it wouldn't be magic.

—⚏—

The world is full of magic things,
patiently waiting for our senses
to grow sharper.

—W.B. YEATS

Clarity

Freedom from confusion

Y EARS AGO, I WAS DESIGN DIRECTOR at a high-tech magazine where I enjoyed creative autonomy and a top-notch salary. According to everyone I should've been thrilled but within a year I was hunting for an escape hatch. *Get me outta here, get me outta here* looped in my head like a bad jingle. I needed more challenge, a job in which my efforts were for more than corporate profit, a career that led to making a direct difference in people's lives. But what that actually meant was an utter mystery.

For two years, I struggled for clarity. I began meditating in earnest. I read find-your-passion books, journaled every day, made lists, talked to friends, even found a therapist—all in search of clues that never came. What to do eluded me until one day, a month before my 40th birthday, my boss plopped himself down in my office and asked me to infiltrate the competition by posing as a job applicant. He wanted me to spy. I leaned back in my chair and felt my mind clear. Goosebumps lifted the hairs on the back of my neck as I fought back a smile. This was it—the sign I'd been waiting for. Unequivocal, sharp as diamond. I had no plan and no money but I knew I was done. Ten days later, I quit.

Clarity can be elusive. Like all inspiration, it has its own agenda, lives on its own timetable. Almost always, answers abhor a struggle. Try too hard and they'll keep their distance. But turn your mind away and the whispers will make themselves heard.

Clarity is never missing. We're just not ready to see it. Guidance, on the other hand, is always there, the itch that pushes you in search of clarity. Follow the guidance and you will find the clarity.

Meditate, pray, write, paint, hike, run, sing, dance. Do whatever it is you do to access your inner wisdom, then listen. You may not like what you hear but it will point toward clarity. Follow the whispered crumbs of guidance. Have faith that the answers you seek are seeking you.

—❧—

What you don't know, you're not
supposed to know yet.

— GLENNON DOYLE

Community

Individuals strengthened by connection

EVERY THURSDAY NIGHT, FOR FIVE years, I've driven across town to sit in a circle of women writers. In word and voice we share our lives—past, present and future, dreams and disappointments. We begin and end to the sound of a singing bowl. We sip tea and pop raspberries as we celebrate births and publishing victories, encourage the disheartened, hold fast to faith when others can't. Together, we bear witness to grief, sit silently when voices crack and always bow in the presence of truth.

For me, this circle has been a beacon in the fog, urging me forward when the road ahead felt dark and impassable. Alone, I am a gossamer-thin thread, but weave me into others and I feel strong and useful like rope—bolstered by the tether.

This is community—the power of communing.

A baby left untended will fail to thrive. Deny the gift of touch and the tender soul will retreat and harden. Human beings need to brush up against one another, to see ourselves reflected in someone else's eyes so we understand who we are.

Behind our computers and cell phones, it's easy to feel alone—each of us on our own island. But we are not alone. At the water's edge, the land at your feet slips beneath the sea and rises again at someone else's shore. Even islands are connected.

—◆—

We have all known the long loneliness, and we have found that the answer is community.

—Dorothy Day

Love

*Affection not subject to
limits or conditions*

MY MOTHER WAS BURDENED WITH a steamer trunk full of troubles: a catalog of phobias, a messy affinity for booze and cigarettes and a natural gift for sarcasm with teeth that could bite. So when the opportunity arose, I put three thousand miles between us and moved from Boston to San Francisco. The chill of the Pacific felt right. Years passed and my resentments grew in lockstep with her general discontent. I often spent our weekly calls listening to her complaints with the phone outstretched, an arm's length away to protect my brain from her vitriol. My mother was, for me, hard to love.

But when she fell and broke her hip at age 79, I jumped on the next plane and spent the six-hour cross-country flight praying for the strength to become the daughter I needed—and wanted—to be. An x-ray taken just before her hip surgery detected lung cancer. I took an indefinite leave from my job and three weeks later had hospice on speed dial.

The last months of my mom's life were a physical, emotional ordeal. My patience was thin; my composure was fragile. But in the midst of her screaming and thrashing and hissing at me like a cornered cat, I discovered something I didn't know I had. To my great surprise, I had a steamer trunk of my own—this one full of love. My years in Al Anon, on therapy couches and stumbling down a spiritual path had borne fruit. As I sat beside her or held a straw to her lips or withdrew the oxygen tubing from her nose so she could smoke another cigarette, I was drawing from an unfamiliar, seemingly bottomless reservoir of patience and goodwill. All the ways she'd fallen short of my expectations, or missed the mark entirely, evaporated and in their place was love—the unconditional variety, the kind uninterested in reciprocity, the kind that forgives and wants only to serve. Whether I had liked her or would have chosen her as a friend was irrelevant. She needed love and I had it to give. I loved her.

If love were a thing it would be like air, invisible, silent and ever-present; as available at a divorce hearing as a wedding; as present on death row as a maternity ward. No mountain is too high, no mistake too glaring, no wound too painful to deter love. But, sadly, we forget. We impose conditions. We wait for tragedies—hurricanes and floods, errant politicians and melting snow caps, people we love who lie sick and dying—to lift our heads and discover our boundless capacity for love.

The night of my mother's death, after draping her tiny

frame in a gauzy-thin white cloth and kissing her fore-head with a final goodbye, I drove to the ocean. I needed to be in a place as big and wild as my feelings. I walked to the water's edge, buried my feet in the warm, wet sand and raised my head to the sky. The ancient Greeks defined seven types of love: love of family, love of friends, love of children, love of physical pleasure, love of play, love of self and love of soul. Standing in the wind that night, they all swarmed in a great storm. The love I felt for my mother was indistinguishable from my love for my wife or myself or the sound of the waves or dancing to Michael Jackson in my pajamas or the charcuterie plate with olives I would soon arrange for Mom's memorial. They were all life, a prize of sweet pollen floating in the air, waiting for an open heart.

—∭—

Your task is not to seek for love,
but merely to seek and find all the
barriers within yourself that you
have built against it.

— RUMI

Creativity

The manifestation of inspiration

I NEVER ASKED TO BE a writer. Designing with color, composition and form was more my game. But, many years ago, a voice inside my head nudged me to the page. The words it whispered needed to be set down so I became a cosmic stenographer, a Gal Friday to the ether. I sat with pen and paper and scooped words out of the air, watching them materialize on the page. For years, I puzzled over where the messages came from. They were, after all, wiser, gentler, smarter than I could ever be. Was it God? A muse? Was there a difference?

After years of waking up in the morning with sentence fragments swirling in my head, I no longer worry about their source. I trust the messages I hear in the wind. Familiar or foreign, lucid or opaque, they float in the firmament, asking to be gathered up and strung together. That's the creator's job—my job.

Often, it's a slog. When the sentences are a snarled mess, my ego swoops down from its nest and pulls back a curtain to reveal an audience. How could I forget? The reader. The judge. The critic. Suddenly everything I write is pretentious or cliche, or has been said before and better by someone else. I want to toss the laptop aside and pick up my camera. *That* I'm good at. But I don't. I plod on, reminding myself that creativity isn't interested in an audience or perfection. Creativity asks only to be expressed—given life.

Like all birthings, creativity is an amalgam of miracle and hard work. The creator's task is to ready the stage, take up their instrument and make themselves available. For me, it is in the pre-dawn hours when the sky is still dark and words hover low above the fresh and fallow fields of my mind. In those precious moments, far from prying eyes, I sit with my fingers poised above the keyboard, open myself to the muse and lay its gifts across the page.

—᠁—

It is only through a human's efforts
that an idea can be escorted out of
the ether and into the realm
of the actual.

—Elizabeth Gilbert

Belonging

The grace of affinity

S HE WAS BLACK, I WAS white and we were lesbians holding hands, walking down a bustling street in racially torn Boston, when a car pulled to the curb and honked. Four young white men in a late-model sedan with whitewall tires eyed us. "Looka' what we got here, fellas," the driver said, his elbow resting casually out the window like he owned the place, an overseer patrolling his plantation. "A little chick-on-chick action."

Our hands flew apart. It was 1982, before being queer was cool.

Another voice, maybe from the backseat. "Yeah, and they're fuckin' salt 'n pepper, and salt 'n pepper don't belong here—not in my neighborhood."

My mouth went dry.

The car shadowed us as we picked up our pace. I lowered my head and watched the cracks in the sidewalk, wondering if anyone on the street would intercede. They didn't.

"Salt 'n pepper? I'd say a shit sundae. Go back where

you belong, college girls."

I wish I could say we'd had the presence of mind to shoot back some piercing retort—claim our right to be what and with whom we wanted—but we didn't. For half a block they continued their taunting. Once they sped off, tires screeching, we stopped and stood slack-jawed. Crowds parted around us as we strained to understand which was our bigger offense—being gay, mixed-race, educated? Which part of us didn't belong?

Heading home on the subway to a neighborhood in the full fury of gentrification, we didn't hold hands but sat close, shoulder to shoulder, hip to hip, never in doubt that we belonged to one another.

We humans are, by nature, a communing bunch. We need one another to raise our children, tend our fields, bury us when we die. We pick and choose, accept and shun, push away and draw close to who, what and where we believe we belong. But beyond kinship and the flags we fly, we belong to one another. All of us. We are like a mobile, individuals strung together by invisible thread, tenuous and fragile, but strong enough to endure the shifting winds.

—∞—

If we have no peace it is because
we have forgotten that we belong
to each other.

—MOTHER TERESA

Openness

Making way for possibility

W<small>E CLOSE OUR WINDOWS AGAINST</small> cold, rain and biting mosquitoes. We lock our doors to keep our possessions safe and privacy intact. We build fences and guard the gate rather than risk the arrival of the stranger. But what if, when we begin each day, we allow ourselves to welcome whatever is to come— friend or foreigner, familiar or not? What if we trusted life and ourselves enough to give new ideas, new experiences, new people the benefit of our attention?

For forty-five years I steered clear of religion. Obedience to something unprovable, not to mention patriarchal, was fool-headed. But when a new friend—a woman I greatly admired—invited me to her "new-thought omni-faith" church (whatever that was), I set my preconceptions aside and climbed in the car.

To my surprise, after only a few minutes in that balcony pew, my biases began crumbling. This wasn't the church I knew from Boston where music lumbered, congregants sat a respectful New England distance apart and the air was laden with thees and thous. Here, the choir roused me to my feet, joy filled the air, and in the message I heard answers to questions I'd been carrying for decades. By the time my friend and I stepped outside into the midday sun, I knew I'd found my new community—a spiritual home I didn't know I'd been missing.

A closed mind is like a race horse trapped at the starting gate—all potential with nowhere to go. To live a life of openness is to meet each day with a willing, curious, trusting heart. To be open is to set our certainty aside, to look beyond ourselves, to sit with someone or something we don't like and search for common ground. To be open is to be present to what life extends—the blank canvas of every sunrise, the crepe-paper sheen on a lake's surface, an invitation to explore an opposing view.

—⁂—

Minds are like parachutes—
they only function when open.

—THOMAS DEWAR

Devotion

Giving one's life wholeheartedly

I
N ART HISTORY CLASS, I fell in love with Mont Saint-Michel, a 10th century Benedictine monastery on the tidal plains of Normandy. Cloistered behind four-foot-thick walls, hundreds of monks in rough hooded robes took vows of poverty, chastity and obedience. They worked the fields, prayed eight times a day, scribed bible verse onto papyrus with pen quill and ink and sacrificed everything—comfort, sleep, time, money, pleasure, family—for their faith. As an aimless college student, I was entranced. The depth of their fervor, their single-mindedness, their willingness to suffer for their beliefs gripped me. Would I ever know such dedication?

Forty years later, I finally find myself seized by a cause that has me in its grip. Like the monks, I rise before dawn, don a robe and begin my devotion—I write. All day, words dance in my head and I corral them into sentences on the page. Every day, for hours, I type, hunched at a laptop until I'm stiff and squinting. When I'm not actually writing,

41

I'm thinking about writing. I forget to eat, forgo weekends, spend money I shouldn't and, like my medieval brothers, sequester myself in my mind, far from those I love, giving my best attention to the page.

There's no halfway with devotion. Whatever we devote ourselves to—whether it be God or gun rights, saving the whales or writing—it takes rigor and commitment, a willingness to persevere regardless of cost. In devotion, sacrifice is required. Like the monks of Mont Saint-Michel, we bow to our calling, hand over our lives and watch as everything else in the world falls away.

—∞—

Devotion is a place where you do
not exist: life flows through you as a
certain sweetness and beauty.

— JAGGI VASUDEV

Curiosity

A beacon alerting us to who we are

I WAS ONCE BEWITCHED BY a Jackson Pollock painting. Across the gallery, it drew me to it like a kid to candy. As other museum visitors cocked their head at the canvas and moved on, I stood mesmerized, feasting on the rivers of paint, splats of color—why orange, why there?—the controlled chaos, the immediacy of his effort. I imagined him in his studio surrounded by buckets of thinned enamel, circling the canvas, arms swinging, cadmium yellow arcing through the air before falling just right. I was a college freshman in search of a future. Could I be an artist?

The questions we ask tell us who we are. The roads down which we wander reveal where we want to go. While I did not become a painter, I spent my college years studying art history and, later, chose graphic design as a career. Filling my eyes with color and composition, form and function would become one of the great pleasures of my life.

The word "curiosity" is, at first glance, light of spirit—more feather duster than sledgehammer. The things we're curious about are sidelines, extracurricular activities, hobbies. But curiosity is the source of all that we create and invent. Curiosity is the fuel that turns the turbine, moves our bodies, propels us into a future with new, different, better possibilities. Jonah Salk was curious about the polio virus, Ghandi was curious about the power of non-violence, Pollock was curious about what would happen if you poured rather than brushed paint.

What piques curiosity is more than a passing fancy—it's the voice of the soul. It speaks to us of who we are, what gives us pleasure, what matters most. Listen, then follow its lead into new worlds of wonder.

—⚡︎—

The flame that burns inside,
the one that nudges you awake at night,
will be the light that guides you home.

—CK

Faith

An abiding trust that comforts

I HAVE A VOICE THAT lives inside me, at the bottom of my ribs, within arm's reach of my heart. When worries and confusion threaten to unhinge me, a wise something speaks in simple, gentle words that tether me to earth. It reminds me that I'm worthy of my dreams, convinces me that everything—yes, everything—is for my good.

The whisper echoes through me, filling me, swaddling me in a warm blanket and holding me fast. For a born-and-raised atheist like me, the source of this comfort is a mystery. Where does such a thing come from? Why did it choose to make a home in me? How can anything be so kind, so patient, so unconditional? The fact of this voice defies logic but rationality and reason lose their allure when I hear its soft words. In my body, I know—without a doubt—that I'm hearing truth; that I'm not alone; that all is well; that I'm strong enough to endure whatever may come.

Tumult is inevitable. Life can be moving along smoothly until a doctor utters the word "cancer." The future feels bright until the phone rings at 4:00 AM and I learn my dear father has died. The ground is stable and sturdy until tectonic plates shift and books start tumbling off shelves onto the floor. Nothing is as solid or dependable as it seems.

Except the voice. My voice. It is immune to the whims and winds of daily life, not fooled by transitory highs. Ever ready, always at hand. A net waiting to catch me. That is faith. Pillow soft and redwood strong.

—⁓—

Faith is the bird that feels the light
when the dawn is still dark.

—RABINDRANATH TAGORE

Presence

Knowing the fullness of the moment

T HERE WAS A CLOCK IN my mother's room at Hospice by the Sea that ran ten minutes fast. Every morning, I'd climb on a chair, pull the clock off the wall and correct the time. Setting things right was the least I could do. When I mentioned the errant clock to the Hospice Chaplain, she smiled, not surprised by my news. "Yes, most of the clocks here run fast. Ironic, isn't it?"

Caring for my mother when she had lung cancer was— among a sea of other lessons—a master class in presence. As we danced with death, rhythms got tangled; in the midst of suffering, time warped. Days blew past while seconds rolled out into hours. Near the end, I'd pull the La-Z-Boy up close and watch her breathe, her chest rising in long, rumbling rolls then falling in gasps of release before going stone still. I'd lean in and wait. Will there be another? After four breaths of my own, I'd shoot a glance at the clock's second-hand and start to count. Twenty, thirty, forty, fifty, sixty—each second stretched and stuffed, each nerve quivering. How long can one go? At seventy seconds, I'd bolt out of my chair. Is this it? Please, let this be the end; oh God, no, not yet. At ninety seconds, with a jagged heave, she'd suck up another breath and with it, another minute of living.

Those last days were the hardest and most precious of my life. As time slipped away for her, it came into focus for me. The tyranny of thinking was set aside, my mind erased of past and future. No anticipation or regret, no judgment or recrimination. That is presence. No concern for the clock, just the pinprick sharp truth of the moment.

—⁓—

In the presence of eternity,
the mountains are as transient as
the clouds.

—ROBERT GREEN INGERSOLL

Freedom

The drive for self-determination

YOLANDA WAS BORN IN THE U.S. but spent her childhood in rural Mexico where there were no schools. Returning to California at fifteen, she stumbled into high school where she was bullied and beaten for not knowing her multiplication tables or how to read or write. She quickly dropped out and learned to survive until landing in my office, ten years later, desperate for a GED and some vocational training. Education could be her ticket to freedom and, as she put it, "to do better than my mother."

Lindsey was born on a farm in Nebraska. From the beginning, her body was wrong, a prison from which there was no escape. There was no ducking out on her boy bones or ignoring the rules that came with how others perceived her. When Lindsey told her parents that God had made "a terrible mistake," a wall of silence rose and life became a penance. As soon as she could, she climbed on a bus and headed for San Francisco where the transgender community offered her refuge. Soon enough, Lindsey was free to walk, work, wear, love, be the woman she'd been all along.

Jan, my father, fled Czechoslovakia in 1948 to escape conscription in the Soviet Army. He expected to return within the year but the iron curtain fell hard and fast, and it would be four decades before he set foot again on Czech soil. While he never regretted his decision to leave, his freedom came with a price—a sadness that always lurked. In spite of a house in the suburbs, a wife and two children, home would always be across the Atlantic in Bohemia. He chose to leave his country, family, land, and language rather than be denied choices. My father valued freedom above all else.

Life is full of obstacles—some self-created, others not of our own making—but there's no quieting the call of our dreams. We sense our promise and long to manifest it. Freedom is that voice inside, whisper or roar, that pushes us past our circumstances and into a field where our potential stands waiting, waving us on to greet the new day.

—⚒—

Is freedom anything else than the
right to live as we wish?
Nothing else.

—Epictetus

Transformation

Being made new

A S FAR BACK AS I can remember, my neck was my albatross. The simple thought of those two sinewy tendons and that globular, bobbing Adam's apple made me recoil. As a kid in bed at night, images of prone throats and glinting knives, guillotines and circular saws assaulted me in wide-screen technicolor until I had to snap on the light. During the day, I learned to adjust. Turtlenecks, a staple in every New England girl's wardrobe, were cringe-inducing as was making out with Billy Horowitz. His mouth honed in on my throat like a hawk stalks prey, pushing me to offer up second base sooner than I would have liked.

For years, I managed my discomfort with avoidance until, in my mid thirties, I found myself on a doctor's examining table, head angled backward as a biopsy needle zeroed in on a bulbous lump at the base of my throat. For me, the thought of cancer was less troubling than the damn needle.

As it happened, the nodule wasn't cancerous but surgery was scheduled. In a numb haze, I surrendered as the blade of my nightmares—this time a scalpel—was drawn across my throat. Two days later, standing in front of my bathroom mirror, I peeled back the bandage, raised my chin and leaned in close, then even closer, marveling at the surgeon's handiwork. I stopped breathing when I realized I wasn't flinching. No wincing, no blanching, no frantic grasping for something else to think about. It was just a scar like any other; a cut that needed tending.

Standing tall in front of the mirror, I took in the fullness of myself and saw someone who had, for decades, been running from little more than a thought. The monster at my throat that had felt so formidable and treacherous was, in fact, nothing but a shadow cast by my own imagination. Only when I was forced to face the fear did it slink away, declawed and impotent.

A turn of the mind and a small corner of my life was transformed. My mother sent me scarves to hide the scar and I wore them at my throat with pleasure. Turtlenecks were back in my closet. In the face of all that needs transforming, it was a small victory but if this could happen, then what else was possible? Might it be that the only thing in our way is our willingness to face the pain and recast the light?

—〰—

It is our own thoughts that hold the key to miraculous transformation.

— MARIANNE WILLIAMSON

Softening

Risking vulnerability

I WAS GATHERING UP MY belongings after my "Spiritual Principles in Action" class when I stuck my foot in my mouth. "I won't be here next week. I'm having surgery." Purse and knapsack zippers went quiet as twenty women stopped what they were doing and turned to stare at me. I should have known. Using the word surgery in a room full of metaphysicians was like calling out the cavalry. They couldn't help but come to my rescue.

"Would you like some prayer?"

Red heat flushed my face as I imagined the wheels of my VW Jetta spitting gravel. But there was no escape. As everyone hustled to encircle me, I closed my eyes, shoved my hands deep in my pockets and tried to corral my face into feigned gratitude. The only thing worse than attention was a prayer chamber. They reminded me of tent revivals I'd seen on TV where preachers spit scripture and congregants swoon in the aisle. Didn't these people know I was an atheist from New England? No one swoons in New England.

Twenty voices rose in unison—a humming beehive of prayer—and my heart went cold. Bits of prayer cut through my grousing. *God, watch over Cathy...guide the surgeon's hand...all will be well.* I stood rigid, sloughing off their kindness like dandruff. But the kindness kept coming, wearing me down.

What if there was nothing to protect against?

I took a deep breath and willed myself to relax, to shed my shell and take it in—to soften. At the bottom of a long exhale, my skin gave way and began to buzz. Pulling my hands from my pockets, I let my arms fall loosely at my sides. A warmth rose inside and soon I found myself swaying in soft, gentle circles, moved by the symphony of kindness composed just for me.

Sometimes it's hard to soften. To bare our soul is to risk shame's sting. But driving home that night, I understood that underneath my hard outer crust was a hungry soul that needed feeding. The armor I polished to a shiny brilliance and donned every day wasn't protecting me from danger. It was keeping me from the very thing I wanted most.

—◊◊—

*Where a strong back and soft front
meet is the brave tender ground
in which to root.*

— JOAN HALIFAX

Generosity

Giving freely with loving intent

I HAVE A DEAR FRIEND who was diagnosed with bone cancer. Months of chemotherapy left her body ravaged, forcing her to conserve her energy for only the most essential life tasks. For Denise, that meant eating, sleeping and, above all else, giving. Last Christmas, in spite of fractured bones and migraines, she embraced her holiday shopping with surprising vigor. She wrapped presents as beautifully as ever, wrote her annual holiday poem and drove through sub-zero temperatures from Winnipeg to South Dakota to be sure the U.S. Postal Service delivered her love on time.

When I unwrapped her gift on Christmas morning, a plume of love rose from the box that lay open in my lap. Nestled in a bed of tissue paper was a necklace that had, I soon realized, been pulled from her own jewelry box. I'd seen her wear it, loose at her neck, bold but casual. The beads of pewter, turquoise, and sea green glass were beautiful but it was the thoughtfulness with which they were offered that struck me mute. In spite of insomnia, back pain and the stem cell transplant to come, she'd managed to find the most precious gift of all—a piece of herself I could hold and carry with me forever.

It's humbling being Denise's friend. Wherever she is—at work, the grocery store, in traffic—I imagine her scanning her surroundings, ever on the lookout for ways to lift people up and brighten their day. Giving is her mindset because loving is her way. Through her friendship, I've learned that generosity isn't about the size of a gift or it's inherent quality—it's the heart with which it is given.

It comes as no surprise to me that Denise's favorite flower is the tulip. Like her, the tulip battles the elements, cracks free of confines, and climbs through darkness to offer the world great gasps of color and exuberance. The tulip, like Denise, asks for nothing in return, just the opportunity to bloom and blossom and give its beauty away.

—៣—

*Attention is the rarest and purest
form of generosity.*

—SIMONE WEIL

Gentleness

The quality of being kind and tender

MY FIRST GRADE TEACHER WAS walking up and down the rows of desks asking each of us to spell a word from *Fun With Dick and Jane*. They were easy—*dog, cat, stop, go, big, small*. Then it was my turn.

"Cathy, spell 'every.'"

Every? My eyes went wide. The word had no meaning, no form, no edges to grab hold of. At my desk, with feet dangling, I dropped my chin and stared into the blue and green plaid of my jumper. I couldn't speak; letters floated unmoored. *Eh vr ee?* Twenty sets of eyes turned on me and red roared up my neck and face as a sinkhole swallowed me whole. In the pin-drop silence, I turned on myself with hard, harsh words: *You're so stupid, so dumb. Say nothing.* I took those words to heart and didn't speak up in school—not willingly—until well into college.

Step on a twig and it will snap; tread on a heart and it will break. Sometimes I wonder who I might have become had someone gently wrapped an arm around my shoulders that day and whispered in my ear, "You're perfect just the way you are—every day, in every way. E-V-E-R-Y." Or better still, what if I'd had the wherewithal to be gentle with myself?

We humans—and the planet we inhabit—are tender, and gentleness is the medicine that heals. A sweet kiss on a skinned knee. Lotion on the hands of an ailing patient. Sun power over shale. When someone is broken, we can pour salt in the wound or prepare a clean bandage and help them to chart a course toward renewal.

Gentleness is acknowledging that life can be brittle and that sometimes a warm, steady presence is enough. Gentleness is witnessing pain and offering loving kindness. Gentleness is a quiet, round, softening force with the singular power to heal.

―᠁―

*There is nothing stronger in the
world than gentleness.*

—HAN SUYIN

Sacredness

The embodiment of the cherished

RIVING EAST ALONG CA-140, WE followed the curve of the Merced River. My wife and I talked amiably, blinking in the diamonds of light that shot off the running water's surface. For miles, we followed the single-lane ribbon of asphalt, through a tunnel of trees, until the road suddenly widened and the sky bloomed broad and bright. The vista before us brought our chatter to an abrupt halt as I took my foot off the gas and instinctively reached down to turn off the radio. This was it. The famous meadow. The frothy mane of water cutting through granite. El Capitan. We'd arrived. Yosemite Valley.

I pulled to the shoulder, compelled to give the setting its due. Climbing out of the car, I shook my head in awe, pressed into silence. Gray pine and manzanita framed the soaring cliffs as prairie hawks banked in the breeze. Standing in the late summer sun, I felt my mind soften and my spirit rise. Scores of other people stood along the roadside, still and quiet. I felt the collective reverence of every person who had ever stood in this spot—from the Miwok Indian to the tourist from Kalamazoo—and exhaled in wonder. But there was more here than physical beauty. Hovering in the air was the praise and wonder of millions. This was sacred ground.

To what do you bow? To whom do you kneel? What we deem sacred is personal. For some, it's a cross, a candle lit at sunset, a prayer rug facing Mecca. For others, it is a string of musical notes…a constellation of stars…a hand held in the dark…a tableau of granite and grass.

In the presence of the sacred, there is no sense-making, no words of explanation—only a wash of humility, a rush of gratitude. In the midst of the sacred, the distance between our humanity and divinity dissolves and, in the union, we come to know the full flower of life's grace.

—∞—

Desert or deluge,
in plenty or naught,
drink from sacred waters
and leaden feet take flight.

— CK

Mindfulness

A purposeful return to the present

M INDS ARE LIKE BEEHIVES, CRAMMED tight, each thought insignificant on its own but, strung together, strong enough to sting or drip honey. In a flash, a mind can rush from rain to gutters to hot tub to the argument last night to regret and onward forever through time and space, redirecting at the slightest breeze until coalescing for a beat before spinning off again.

This is the mind's nature. The present is never compelling enough, never good enough. There's always something shiny on the periphery waving us over—goodies in the refrigerator, breaking news, unread books, garden weeds, mistakes and memories to chew on and bask in. We swipe screens and fill our minds with other people's stories rather than attend to our own.

Mindfulness is the conscious decision to stop and rise above the buzzing. When we're mindful we turn away from the noise and take note of ourselves. We become curious. Where am I? What am I doing? Who am I being?

In mindfulness we mind our mind because the life we think about is the life we live. In mindfulness we notice the still fullness of the moment—me on the patio writing, my partner napping inside, cool air on my ankles, a Saturday afternoon in May, a chickadee balanced on the birdfeeder as bees hum in wisteria.

—◊◊◊—

Live the actual moment.
Only this actual moment is life.

– THÍCH NHẤT HẠNH

Abundance

An overflowing supply

LIKE COUNTLESS OTHER LATIN AMERICAN men of his generation, my father-in-law wore a mustache—white and thin with a blunt, bottlebrush edge. I always thought of that mustache as a nod to his imagined machismo. After all, tango dancers require mustaches and he danced tango. But, really, Mauricio was a softie, a warm-hearted doctor who tended to poor families until he was 92 years old. Every day he trimmed his mustache and clipped his beeper to his belt because every day his beard grew and every day his patients needed him. Day after day, life coursed onward.

When he got cancer and went into hospice, I flew to Cleveland. From the airport, I drove to his bedside and sat at his feet for a day before his beautiful life came to an end. Afterward, a handful of us sat with his body and told quiet stories. We met with the rabbi, made arrangements as one does, and two days later, cried at the funeral as Mauricio's spirit gathered in the rafters before moving on.

We went on as he went on. With his body to dust and his soul to flying those of us who loved him gathered in grief. Flowers stood tall in clear crystal vases. Kids played in the hallway and grown-ups piled their plates high with bagels, lox and fruit salad. Four people told me they were alive because Mauricio had saved their life.

Even in death, life is ever flowing—as available as air, as inevitable as pain, as enduring as the sun and moon and sun again. This is abundance.

Hardwired for survival, we tend to notice what's missing. Will there be enough money, time, love, food, chocolate? Scarcity presses in on us but, the truth is, everything we value most is bountiful. Mauricio's sweet heart may be gone but his kindness lives on in all of us. Joy may feel scarce but it is, in fact, inextinguishable. Hope…peace…beauty may appear fleeting but they can't disappear any more than life can stop its forward dance. Look anywhere—outside any window, a corner of cityscape, a patch of sky. Life is forever shining, eternally waving, even from the rafters.

—∞—

Abundance is not something we acquire.
It is something we tune into.

—WAYNE DYER

Serenity

A state of being untroubled and at peace

THERE IS A SPOT IN the Marin Headlands that is, in my memory, mine. I found my hideaway one day when, in a moment of boldness, I shimmied through a hole in a fence and followed a path groomed by deer. I clambered down a crumbling gully, traveling through a grove of manzanita until the narrow path disappeared and the sky opened. In front of me was a hill of tall, waving grasses. I waded upward, through the knee-high ochre, until, out of breath, I crested the hill, scanned the horizon and stopped in my tracks. There, horizon to horizon, was a sweeping vista of San Francisco Bay—from Sausalito to the hills of Berkeley to Alcatraz and the Golden Gate Bridge. At my feet were a million people. Spewing buses, honking cars, cable cars full of tourists. Falafel, moo shu pork, pizza. All the sounds and smells of a city yet there on my grassy headland was silence. Nothing but the brush of wind and pelicans cruising the sweet, salty currents of the Pacific.

Nothing stills my mind or softens my heart like a view.

Within sight of vastness, perspective sets in. I become right-sized, one soul among millions, each of us putting one foot in front of the other. All my mind's striving, the doubting, the worrying goes quiet.

I return often to that bluff because in that spot my mind is calm. Peace settles in. Serenity is mine. But what I know is that that serenity doesn't live in the grasses of that breezy Marin hilltop. Serenity doesn't hide in a gopher hole, waiting for me to show up so it can pop out and express itself. No. I bring the serenity with me. Even in the midst of life's mayhem we have the capacity to call serenity forth, to lift our head above the clouds and feel the warm sun on our face.

—∞—

Serenity is not freedom from the storm;
it is peace within the storm.

– ALCOHOLICS ANONYMOUS

Gratitude

*An appreciation for all that was,
is and will be—regardless*

ROUND THE TABLE SAT REPUBLICANS and Democrats, fundamentalist Christians and avid atheists, capitalists and socialists. Among them was an alcoholic, a teetotaler, a professor, a video gamer, two smokers, two lesbians and three immigrants. My family—a collection of seemingly mismatched people exerting enormous energy to avoid disaster. We dodge subjects like a soldier dodges bullets.

But on that third Thursday of November, after the cut-crystal bowls had been pulled out of hiding and the turkey was plated, we sat down and set our differences aside. No talk of politics or religion or the real story behind the meeting of Indians and Pilgrims. Instead, one by one, we went around the table and spoke words of thanksgiving. Each in our own way, we turned our minds away from our bruises and toward all that had blossomed. We gave voice to what worked, what brought us joy and satisfaction, to what and whom we loved.

We practiced gratitude.

And in that simple act, the threads that bound us, the ones that sometimes felt frayed and ready to break, were made stronger. The eight of us—disparate characters floating unmoored through choppy waters—became a powerful flotilla, bound together by seaworthy rope.

Gratitude is among the strongest forces in the world but, in the midst of trouble, it can be hard to conjure. Drama is all-encompassing but when we're able to see past the pain, the gifts are there, winking at us from the corner. Hardship is never welcome. No one asks for divorce or cancer or bombs or a loved one's death. But trouble always comes and, as we sift through the rubble, we get to choose what to look for. To practice gratitude is to consciously search for treasures.

In gratitude, we are like a sunflower turning to the sun even when it's raining. In gratitude, we don't argue with what fate has delivered. We look through the circumstance for the blessing, the silken bud in the snow.

—❧—

*We can complain because roses have
thorns, or rejoice because thorns
have roses.*

—ALPHONSE KARR

Kindness

Generosity of spirit

Y EARS AGO, I WALKED INTO a bakery and bought a cookie. Strolling down the street, savoring the crunchy walnuts and gooey chocolate chips, I came upon a homeless man sitting cross-legged on the sidewalk, picking at his wiry beard. At his feet was a piece of cardboard that read, "HUNGRY." I flushed and slipped my treat in my coat pocket as I strode past him, chastizing myself for my selfishness. When I turned the corner, safely out of sight, I pulled the cookie from my pocket and took another bite but what had once been sweet was now only bitter.

Homelessness is common in my town. Young addicts, alcoholics and the mentally ill dig through dumpsters, and sleep under plastic sheeting rigged to chain link fences in roadside encampments. It hurts to see their pain, to acknowledge the inequity and feel our power-lessness. So, we walk on by. We avert our eyes and, in the process, deepen the damage—to them and us.

I believe we humans are kind by nature. It's who we are. Our hearts are made to love, to care for one another, to mend what is broken. To turn away from someone's suffering—while understandable—is to dampen our humanity.

Kindness is, in the end, simple. To offer the hungry man my cookie would have been easy enough. While the gesture would have done little to lessen his broader troubles, the quiet act of kindness would have delivered me one step closer to an open heart and offered him a no doubt rare glimpse of hope.

—※—

No act of kindness,
no matter how small,
is ever wasted.

—AESOP

Grace

Manifestation of the universe's benevolence

FOR FIFTEEN YEARS I CLIMBED the ladder of success only to find it leaning against the wrong building. As design director at a thriving technology magazine, I had a six-figure salary, corner office and a belly full of caged birds. I wanted out. No matter how rich the paycheck, making internet protocols look pretty was not my life's calling. I had a soul to attend to, a world to save. But doing what?

A shelf of find-your-passion books offered little advice other than have faith and take a leap, both of which felt more dangerous than helpful. Would faith pay my rent? But after years of feeling trapped, I took the advice and jumped. With no plan, no prospects, no savings, I quit.

Five days into my unemployment, I was on my knees resurrecting a long-neglected garden when the phone rang and grace arrived. An old colleague I barely knew offered me a job. At first I declined. I'd wanted out of the design racket, not back in. But he was dogged and I listened. I'd be a consultant with full autonomy and could work part-time on my own schedule. "Think it over," he said. "Name your price." I glanced at the stack of bills on my desk. Who was this guy?

I spent the weekend with a calculator and on Monday morning I picked up the phone and asked for the biggest number I dared utter—the amount I'd need to pay my bills for a year. He didn't blanch.

As it happened, the project went flawlessly. What we'd thought would take six months took three. By spring I was free to hike the Marin Headlands and contemplate my path forward. I'd stand on rocky outcroppings at the edge of the Pacific, watch the pelicans ride the currents and marvel at the freedom that had, somehow, been delivered to my doorstep. But by whom? By what?

Some would call it God; some would call it luck. I knew it to be grace. The timing was too perfect, the taste in my mouth too sweet to not be from the heavens. I'd taken a deep breath and dared to jump. Only then, as I fell through thin, empty air, did I discover the net that would catch and hold me fast.

—⚬—

I do not at all understand the mystery of grace—only that it meets us where we are but does not leave us where it found us.

—ANNE LAMOTT

Paradox

The bounty of contradiction

M Y MOTHER WAS AS FIERCE and irascible at her death as she had been in life. Her last few months were spent in bed, trapped by lung cancer and a broken hip she'd had rebuilt but refused to rehabilitate. When she wasn't hollowed out and sleeping, she was thrashing in her sheets and screaming in a voice sharp enough to cut bone. For sixty-eight days, with the help of hospice, I stood at her bedside lighting her cigarettes, riding out her hallucinations, pinning her to the mattress to force morphine under her tongue. Those were the hardest, most harrowing days of my life.

They were also the most beautiful.

At the end of each day, when Mom was finally sleeping soundly, I slipped outside into the salty Florida air and took long, deep breaths, releasing the panic I'd been keeping at bay. Leaning my elbows on the patio railing, I peered into the night and took in the moon rising through the cypress grove, felt the southerly breeze, listened to laughter spilling out from neighbors' windows. In spite of all our suffering, life was full of joy and comfort.

The night she died, I went to the beach. It was nearly midnight and a storm to the north was stirring the sea into a tumult of swells and crashes. My mother hadn't been easy but I'd loved her. Our road together had been turbulent yet I'd showed up in full-hearted service, offering her kindness when she needed it most. That night, standing at the warm water's edge with palm fronds clapping in the wind, I befriended paradox. I came to know that we are most alive when pain lives next to joy, when grief and gratitude breathe the same air. I understood that life is at its most vibrant when we open our arms and embrace the contradiction.

—☙—

All the art of living lies in the fine
mingling of letting go and holding on.

—HAVELOCK ELLIS

Hope

The dream, desire and declaration of
a better future

RECENTLY, IN MY CAPACITY AS a career advisor at a public agency, I facilitated a workshop for unemployed folks in Silicon Valley. In the front row was Jonathan, a talented engineer who was homeless, pushing sixty and living in his Toyota Sienna. "I get interviews," he reported, "but the second they see the grey in my hair, I'm finished."

Behind him was Maya, a financial analyst who drove a car with 270,000 miles and an engine light that had been flashing for a year. Every morning she put the key in the ignition, gripped the steering wheel and prayed to Shiva it would start. Her skills were exemplary but in person she struggled. Maya had Asperger's and it showed.

Across the aisle was Deb, a curriculum developer on her fourth career. Unlike Maya, she had no trouble landing jobs. Her problem was they were all short-term contracts with no benefits. She was single and 63. "That's the way it is now," she said bitterly. "I'm an itinerant laborer with a master's degree."

Sitting at the front of the room, I listened as powerlessness spread among my clients like a virus, infecting me along the way. Everything they railed against was real—discrimination, corporate greed, globalization. Society was crumbling. Civility was dead. Wall Street was winning and always would. I hung my head, staring at the linoleum. I had nothing—nothing to say, nothing to offer. They were right, we were doomed.

But wait. Stop. These were talented people and I was paid to be positive, to offer up job search advice with a heaping tablespoon of optimism. So I dug deep and offered up the shortest prayer I knew—*Help*. Images of the brave students who survived the latest school shooting flashed in my mind. Just because people think they're powerless doesn't mean they are. We don't have to stop trying just because it gets hard.

I raised my head and cleared my throat. "Listen up," I said, intent on reeling the conversation back from the brink. "I get it. The cards are stacked. The world is a wreck and being unemployed sucks. But here's what I know. You're smart, hardworking, capable people. Companies would be lucky to have you." The room went quiet, their eyes hungry. Compliments are scarce when you're unemployed so they drank with a thirst. "You can't give up. You can't cave. You have to remember who you are. You have to hold onto hope."

My words hung in the air. My face flushed. Had I just become a Hallmark card? Spewing platitudes was easy; I had a job. But I looked around the room and saw them nodding, their faces brighter. The energy had shifted and, ten minutes later, when they filed out of the classroom, they stood a little taller, eyes focused forward.

HOPE CAN FEEL IMPOSSIBLE—even harebrained and irresponsible—when so much in our world is confused and broken. Hope and despair are sisters; they come together. The problems are overwhelming, a flood of troubled waters rushing too fast to navigate. But to give up on hope is to let the river take us where we don't want to go.

To hope is to lay claim to the future we want. Whether it's a steady job, a bicycle under the Christmas tree or world peace, to hope is to declare the world we want to inhabit. It's a small word with big power. It's the animating force that propels people to cross oceans, to re-invent themselves, to start businesses, propose marriage, make babies, vote, create, wake at the crack of dawn to write books.

In hope, we risk disappointment. It takes patience and, as we wait for what we want, our well may run dry. So we rest, gather our strength, ask for help and keep going because there's always more hope if we're brave enough to keep digging.

—∿—

Hope is being able to see that there is light despite all the darkness.

— DESMOND TUTU

Tenderness

A feeling or act of gentle kindness

P EERING THROUGH MY WINDSHIELD, I spotted what looked to be a girl, seven or eight years old, wearing bright white tights, racing her bicycle up the middle of the road. She was up on her feet, leaning into the handlebars, shoulders pitching left and right, her sneakers pumping the pedals as if chased by a rabid dog. Where was she going in such a fury? It was dawn, too early for school, too dark for a kid to be out alone. And why was she wearing a down jacket with the hood pulled up tight over her head? It was late August. Something wasn't right, something was off about those tights.

When the pitch of the hill slowed her pace, I passed her on the left and shot a looked in my rear view mirror. Out from beneath the bill of a ballcap glowed a face as white as paper. Alabaster white. Bone china white. Albino white. I leaned into the mirror and blinked as my assumptions fell away. This wasn't a girl but a boy. He wasn't running from anything; he was having fun. Those weren't tights, they were skin.

I slowed the car, peering at him in the mirror as compassion swelled in my chest. I imagined him on a playground—teased and taunted, an easy target for bullies. For life, his body would be a curiosity for others to ogle. I wanted to scoop him up, take him home and make him cocoa.

At the next corner, he turned and rode out of sight as my mind slipped into fantasy. If he were mine, I'd wake him every morning with gentle kisses and sweet endearments. Before he left for school I'd cradle his face in my hands and remind him he was perfect just the way he was. At night, I'd tuck him into bed and sing him lullabies until he was fast asleep and safe from harm.

As the street light turned red, I reached for a tissue. *Why was I so moved?* Three blocks later, I remembered—I'd once been an object of derision myself. A mouth full of horrid, misdirected teeth inspired pointing and jeering. For years I heard, "Hey Bucky, where's the carrot?" My frailty had been on full display—a defect in flashing neon—and I had no one at home able to hug me tight and tell me I was beautiful just the way I was. Sadly, my parents were ill-equipped to even notice I was slowly learning to hate myself.

Oral surgery and five years of braces later, my teeth were fixed but the pain had taken root. Merging onto the highway that morning, it dawned on me that I was now a strong and confident woman with the capacity to kneel down with my pain, look myself in the eye and be kind. I could hold my face in my hands, soften my voice and be tender with the parts of me that, at times, still hurt.

—〰—

Our greatest strength lies in the
gentleness and tenderness of our heart.

— RUMI

Voice

An instrument of the soul

R AISED BY ALCOHOLICS, I LEARNED early to scan for danger. I mastered the art of reading other people's moods, then fulfilling their needs while silencing my own. For decades, obfuscation worked until I found myself in mid-life, unemployed and alone in a new city, spinning in the backwash of a bitter breakup. With family and friends three thousand miles away, I was adrift. With no one to fill the vacuum, I began to hear something I'd never heard before. From deep inside came a murmur, a soft, gentle whisper that, to my surprise, loved me without reservation.

We all have inner voices. But, sadly, they're not all kind. All too often, the song I hear in my head is dissonant and biting. The lyrics speak of shame and shortcomings, what's missing and wrong. But when I'm able to get quiet and still, I can detect a more melodious tune. When I listen more deeply—past the task master and ill-tempered judge—I find a kind golden sage with benevolence at its core.

Is it the soul? God? Intuition? Wisdom earned over time? Regardless of what you call it or where it comes from, we know it when we hear it. We feel it in our bodies. A softening of the brow, a rush of goosebumps, a yearning in our belly that won't loosen it's grip. No matter its language, this inner voice knows no wrong, is incapable of harm and wants nothing but our fulfillment. That's the voice to follow and heed. Recognize its intent, learn its vocabulary. Attend to its message.

Words matter. Our voice—including the one we use to speak, connect, share our thoughts and feelings—has the power to do great good or great harm to ourselves and others. We can vilify or praise. We can use technology to sow division or build bridges. Allow the grace of our inner voice to inform the outer and its whisper just may become the song the world most needs to hear.

—⚊—

Underneath all that we are taught,
there is a voice that calls to us
beyond what is reasonable, and in
listening to the flicker of spirit, we
often find deep healing.

– MARK NEPO

Flow

Movement in a steady, continuous stream

THE INTRACOASTAL WATERWAY IS A 3,000-mile inland marine highway—part natural, part man-made—that runs down the eastern seaboard from Boston to Miami, right past me in my pajamas as I sip sweet tea in an apartment in Deerfield Beach, FL. I inherited the condo from my mother who inherited it from her parents who retired to this piece of the tropics in 1964 after a long, fruitful life in New York City.

As water flows, so does time.

Twice a year, I fly cross-country to vacation in Florida. I tell myself I go for the beach, the vitamin D buzz I get from the sun and to watch boats pulled and pushed by the invisible currents and steady tides. But the truth is, with the house I grew up in gone, that apartment is as close to home as I can get. The memories it holds—some lovely, many not—place me on a timeline. Standing in the living room, I scan the shelves of the glass-fronted display cabinet and see the continuance of time: my grandparents' silver-plated cigarette box, a Czech crystal platter from my father's cousin, a framed photograph of my mother at eighteen—beautiful and full of promise in a white chiffon gown and pearls. Next to the picture is an unadorned charcoal gray box that holds all that remains of her body.

Everything evolves; nothing is static. Minutes become hours become days become generations spreading into millennia. Like water rushing over rocks, time moves forward, pushing past obstacles, uninterested in our stories, no matter how loudly they roar.

The world through which time flows often feels full of trouble. Institutions are crumbling, people go hungry, history gets forgotten, skin color still divides. Even Earth, as powerful as she is, isn't immune. Soon, sea levels will rise and the briny waters of the Intracoastal will be lapping onto the second-floor patio where I sit and watch the cabin cruisers putter by.

But every morning brings a new day, a new river made of new choices. I can sit on the seawall and write or swim with the manatee or hitch a ride on a catamaran and head for Biscayne Bay and the Caribbean beyond. Either way, with every breath, a fresh future arrives—ours to forge. This is flow.

—❧—

No man ever steps in the same river twice,
for it is not the same river and
he is not the same man.

— HERACLITUS

Surrender

A yielding of control

SOME SAY THAT ONLY COWARDS surrender. I say that sometimes the bravest thing we can do is refuse to fight. I'm married and my wife seems, at times, to have descended from another planet. Mostly our differences bring us together but occasionally they push us apart. When tensions flare, I pull up the drawbridge, pace in my office where I craft arguments that prove I'm the victim and she's the villain. Fueled by righteousness, I fume and ready my verbal cannons.

But, time passes. Adrenalin levels drop, cortisol cools and I remember what I know—that true healing comes in the staying, in the listening, even when it stings. Through my dissipating anger I remember that being right—or wrong—isn't worth the cost of being alone, now or forever. So I put down my ax and go find her.

There are fights worth fighting. As long as there is injustice, as long as there are people suffering, there are battles worth waging. The question is, what weapons do we bring to the fight? A knife or an open ear, armor or a softened heart, a battalion or a lone voice that speaks with conviction? We assume war is inevitable but what would happen if everyone everywhere climbed out of their trenches and raised a white flag? Who would win? Wouldn't everyone?

Sometimes surrendering leads to winning. Caterpillars surrender their cocoon, trees surrender their leaves, a wife intent on healing surrenders her sword. To surrender is to let go of what is and welcome something new. Like the leaf floating on the river that yields to the rock, when we surrender we submit to the current, trusting it will take us where we need to go.

—⚡—

Surrender is the simple but profound
wisdom of yielding to rather than
opposing the flow of life.

—ECHKART TOLLE

Peace

Freedom from strife

A T NIGHT, MY PARENTS FOUGHT. Vodka-laced arguments floated up the heating vent into my bedroom where I lay holding my breath, listening to my mother's verbal blows and my father's dark silence. In my mind, he was cowering, caught in the circle of light cast by a desk lamp as my mother stomped between kitchen and den, spewing her disappointments while cigarette smoke snaked up her arm. Upstairs, knees tight to my chest, I stared unblinking at the shadows, desperate to not hear the front door slam as my mother stormed off into the night.

By morning, in the sober light of day, all was forgotten. Mom and Dad sat side-by-side on the couch, sipping tea, chatting amicably about some story they'd read in the *New York Times*. Somehow Vietnam body counts and the havoc of Watergate brought peace to my family.

In the calm of those armistices, I could breathe again. I sat cross-legged at their feet and flipped through *Travel & Leisure*, safe enough for the moment to dream of biking through Scotland or cruising down the Yangtze River. In those windows of peace, before cocktail hour struck at 5:00, I was free to run outside and play, climb trees and listen to doves cooing.

Fear is stifling. In the midst of battle, large or small, our focus narrows. With too much strife, we can't think clearly—the din too loud, the walls too close. We contract and fortify ourselves for what's next—survival or revenge, safety or rupture. But in times of peace, we're able to make choices, imagine a future, create art, enjoy the sensory pleasures of life: a summer peach, the scent of honeysuckle. In peace, we're free to express ourselves fully, to trust, to open our hearts wide enough to love big, even those who threaten the very peace we enjoy.

—ᴍ—

Without peace of mind, life is just a
shadow of its possibilities.

—Joan Borysenko

Transcendence

Rising above the physical to the sublime

THE WOODEN SLATS CREAKED UNDER foot as I walked to the railing and peered out over rooftops to the lightening sky in the east. Most of the apartment windows were still dark and, as dawn broke, I wondered how many people across the city were making love. Did they know how lucky they were? The rickety deck, aged by the fog that rolled up San Francisco Bay, used to be our romantic refuge. We'd sit in mismatched chaises, watch the stars come out and make plans. Not anymore.

The previous evening, as I poked at gravel in the street with a stick, Judit broke up with me. "I'm sorry," she'd said. "I just can't do this. Not now." My mind went dull grey as a loose manhole cover convulsed under the wheels of a passing bus.

The next morning, I leaned my belly against the deck's wooden railing. As the sun filigreed the edges of the clouds waiting at the horizon, I lifted my face to the sky, closed my eyes and took long, deep breaths. I imagined Judit asleep, a hand tucked tidily under her face. *I will not be loved by her, not today, not ever again.* I thought of all the empty weekends to come, reading the Sunday newspaper alone, the trips we'd imagined that would never come to pass. As memories of past lovers and lost friends rushed in, I let the river take me. Tears streamed down my face into the dark garden below. My heart was, for the first time, truly broken.

But then, out of the roar of the flood, I heard a simple, quiet thought:

"You are lucky to have loved so deeply."

Wait.

What?

I released my grip on the railing and looked up to see rays of the risen sun shooting through the clouds. The bay was shimmering in morning light. It was true. I hurt so much because I loved so much. Wasn't a heart full of love a blessing? With that, the world changed color and heaviness flew from my chest.

SOMETIMES A WINDOW OPENS. In spite of everything, the gauzy curtain is blown aside and on the breeze we catch a glimpse of something fresh, something important, something that changes everything for the better. Transcendence—a moment when we climb beyond our earthly concerns into the heavens where truth sits patiently, waiting.

And in those moments, if we dare, we pull up a seat, open our hungry hearts and minds—and listen.

—∞—

What we resist persists.
What we think and feel we make real.
What we befriend we transcend.

—CK

Intuition

The perception of truth in our bodies

WITH GOOGLE, ANSWERS ARE AT our fingertips—literally. How many tablespoons in a cup? Who played the matriarch on "Big Valley"? How many people go to bed hungry? A few clicks later we have our answers. (16; Barbara Stanwyck, 800 million) But what if our questions are more nuanced and beyond the reach of a digital cloud server? Should I marry him? Move to Vancouver? Change careers?

I once had a job that should've been perfect. Good company, booming industry, corner office. I was paid well and had full autonomy yet I woke up every morning with an ache inside me spreading like a bruise. Something wasn't right. I was meant for more. I needed out. This I knew because my gut told me so.

Intuition uses no words. It speaks through the body: a roil in the belly, a tingle in the bones, the hum of whispering angels in our ear. The insight may come in a hard flash that leaves us mute and blinking or it can settle under the surface, dormant and dull, capable of unerring patience. Its message may not always be welcome—change often isn't—but it is incapable of deception or malevolence. Its goal is singular and pure—for us to live our best life.

Our task is to create enough stillness to hear beyond our mind's chattering and the bellowing of other people's opinions. We must cultivate our ability to discern and to trust our intuition's good intentions, then love ourselves enough to accept its invitation.

—∞—

"Listen to the wind, it talks.
Listen to the silence, it speaks.
Listen to your heart, it knows."

—NATIVE AMERICAN PROVERB

Vulnerability

The choice to risk being seen

THERE ARE FEW THINGS I hate as much as being laughed at. But, sadly, as a kid too consumed by family chaos to detect my own body's needs, I had lots of practice. I threw up in seventh grade social studies and in line at the commissary at Camp Mohawk and in the shoe department at Filene's. When called on by teachers I'd go mute then scarlet-red. I peed in my shorts while doing jumping jacks in third grade gym. Humiliation and I were frequent companions. I learned to hide in plain sight, stay quiet, bury my secrets in the basement where no one, including me, could find them. There they stewed, behind boxes of Christmas tree ornaments and easy lies: *I'm good, how are you?*

Shame is a cloud that dampens the spirit. It's an invisible beast that feeds off silence. Keep small and quiet, I figured, and no one would notice me. But, over time, the secrets I kept didn't fade, they festered. They hurt until I came to understand—with lots of help—that speaking the truth was my ticket out of the basement. I learned that by sharing what cut the deepest, I could slay the monster.

Many years ago, when being gay could still land you in jail, I stepped up to a microphone at a personal development seminar and told two hundred people I was a lesbian. Walking off the stage that afternoon, I was trembling, astounded by my uncharacteristic courage. But even more shocking was the applause and standing ovation I received. For the rest of the weekend, strangers approached me wanting to congratulate me, thank me, hug me. They pulled me aside and, in hushed voices, unburdened themselves by sharing some long-held secret of their own.

By being vulnerable, I'd connected. By dropping my mask and exposing a raw truth, I'd unwittingly thrown a lifeline to everyone in the room who might be drowning. By being honest, I'd given others permission to do the same.

Coming out so publicly was revelatory but my confession didn't put me in any real danger. I was fortunate. My audience was, for the most part, friendly. Plus, I'd been inching the closet door open for six years before kicking it down entirely. That's not always the case. Sometimes wounds are too deep and need gentle care, offered in private. After all, there's no need to bare our throat to the wolf. But, most of the time—for me, anyway—the most menacing wolf in the room is the one in my head.

Shame still shadows me. The memory of urine running down my leg and everyone laughing still stings. I imagine it always will. People struggle and stumble. Nerves fray, bodies fail, façades shatter, classmates laugh and shame burns. But I know now that the more I expose my warts, the less burdensome they become. The more I open my heart and share my frailties and missteps, the more I see them *not* as proof of my weakness but as evidence of my strength.

—⚘—

Like facets on a diamond,
the cuts are what catch the light
and shine so bright.

—CK

Contentment

Satisfaction with what one is or has

S OMETIMES CONTENTMENT FEELS IMPOSSIBLE. Yesterday my computer crashed, I spent an hour at the DMV, got stuck in rush-hour traffic, overcooked the chicken then turned on the news to hear of another gunman unleashing his fury, this time on a baseball game in Virginia. By the time the sun set, my thinking had gone stark, my perspective lost to the events of the day. Life was scratchy and ill-fitting. I needed a makeover, a therapist, a cabin in back-country Montana where I could move and take up fishing.

But then I stopped my careening mind, stepped outside, took a breath, looked up at the stars and remembered what I know. I am more than what happens.

We are what we think about. I once heard a man speak about the peace and freedom he found in prison. His body might have been incarcerated but his spirit was his to command. With bleakness all around, he chose where to put his mind. Twenty-three years in a concrete box and he chose contentment.

All may not be perfect. We are surrounded by messages crafted to convince us we need more to be enough. Sometimes deep wounds cast long shadows. But past all that we perceive to be missing, past all the pains that may plague us, is a pearl of rightness.

Contentment is a place inside where we can sit in the shade of an elm, feel a tender breeze, listen to birds and breathe easy. Contentment is ours to experience when we choose to look past circumstances to the gift that is waiting for us—the gem of life itself.

—∞—

Be content with what you have;
rejoice in the way things are.

When you realize there is nothing
lacking, the whole world
belongs to you.

— LAO TZU

Truth

Accordance with reality

FOR FORTY YEARS I TOLD the story of an idyllic childhood. It was all Coppertone and striped beach towels, sky-high piles of pungent autumn leaves and soaring across a frozen pond on my father's shoulders as Mom's hot chocolate with mini-islands of marshmallow waited for me at home. I told that story because it was true. I was adored and indulged, cared for and loved.

But there's another story, one just as true but not as glistening. In that account, I lie in bed at night terrified by the screaming downstairs; I suck my thumb until I do damage to my teeth; I am prescribed a medicine to entice me to eat; and every night I get a funny, queasy feeling in my belly when cocktail hour arrives and everything changes. In that story, I think myself ugly and make it my job to make myself invisible. That's a story I never told, much less allowed myself to feel. Why would I?

Because—I eventually learned—telling half truths doesn't work. For decades, I walked through life covered in bruises I didn't know I had, wondering why everything I touched hurt. But now, thanks to countless teachers, I understand—or at least am beginning to. Like rain sculpts sandstone and fire levels forests that rise again even stronger, all that I have endured has shaped me. To deny the thorn is to diminish the rose.

Truth is, of course, a fickle master. There are no absolutes. Like beauty, it is in the eye of the beholder. History gets rewritten; morality shifts in cultural winds; even a rock, in all its solidity, can be transformed into sand. Yet we know truth when we feel it. Goosebumps rise, tears well and a light turns on inside that reveals a vista, vast and waiting. The unabridged story of my childhood—my full truth— may be messy but with its honest telling comes relief and freedom.

—⁊⁊⁊—

Honesty is the first chapter
in the book of wisdom.

— THOMAS JEFFERSON

Wholeness

*A harmonious state in which
everything is present and welcome*

M Y FRIEND PLACED HER NAPKIN in her lap. "Can we pray?"

I twitched and dropped my fork, the clang reverberating like a spade hitting stone. Here? Now? We were having lunch at a university eatery, surrounded by faculty and administrators. *Pray? Right. Sure. Of course.*

I shouldn't have been surprised. She and I had become friends at a spiritual community in California where we were training to be metaphysicians. Before joining this community, I'd considered myself an atheist. Praying was for, well, suckers. Not anymore. Praying had become a tool to recalibrate my mind, to connect with consciousness. But pray out loud? In public? Encircled by PhDs? Didn't she know these people would assume we were Bible-thumpers and hate us?

I scooted my chair forward and reached for her outstretched hands as I split in two. The tables around us suddenly felt as tight as the front pews on Easter Sunday. As she bowed her head and closed her eyes—"Dear Sweet Spirit"—I kept mine wide open, focused on my plate. If the men at the next table happened to glance over, maybe I could throw my friend under the bus with an eye roll. But then I heard my name woven into her prayer, "... Cathy is a blessing ..."

I dropped my chin to my chest and forced my eyes closed. With the world shut away, I climbed inside and found that other part of me—the part I keep to myself, the piece I value most but share the least, the me that lights a candle every morning, curls up on a couch and prays out loud in a clear, unapologetic voice. Across the table, I gave her hands, as smooth and sweet as her words, a gentle squeeze.

Straddling worlds can be exhausting. Inside each of us are disparate parts with sometimes warring voices. We know our tribe's stripes, the cable news they watch, the bumper stickers they affix to their cars. It's easier to be among our own kind. But what happens when we like two different worlds—the mountains and the city, the atheist's garret and the chapel pew? If we love them both, to whom do we pledge our loyalty? Which garden do we feed, water and weed?

Maybe we don't have to choose. Maybe we can be whole. Maybe we can build a trail between the mountains and the city, a place where professors and priests—astrophysicists and astrologers—can meet at night, look up into the darkness and wonder together where the stars sprang from. Maybe, if we're brave, we can open our hearts, be at home in multiple worlds and share all of ourselves.

—∞—

> *Wholeness is not achieved by cutting*
> *off a portion of one's being but by*
> *integration of the contraries.*

—CARL JUNG

Joy

Tapping the infinite well of delight

I ONCE WATCHED A LITTLE girl in a hot pink bathing suit play at the ocean's edge. With lime green floaters on her arms and POWER GIRL written across her chest, she chased the receding water. When the next crest fell, she squealed in delight, spun in mid-air and raced up the sand, hands flapping as the white foam bubbled at her feet. Over and over and over, she played with the surf, never tiring of its magic.

Unlike us, Power Girl had no electric bill to pay, no career to worry about, no exes to navigate, no past or future to catalogue and review. Without responsibilities, she was free to embody the pleasure of the moment. Not us grownups. Our minds are too full to find joy. But despite all that we tell ourselves—all our habits and expectations—joy is always available, waiting for us to take notice.

Often, it arrives unbeckoned. I can be in the kitchen peeling potatoes, tired and cranky, when a piece of music I love comes on the radio. Soon my toes are tapping, my dreary thoughts are gone and, before I know it, the Yukon

Golds are sidelined and I'm dancing in the living room like John Travolta. To my surprise, joy was right there all along.

There's joy in that first sip of coffee in the morning, in the angle of the mid-summer sun, in memories of my wedding day. Just this morning, I was reading the newspaper, fuming over another story of political malfeasance when Lilly the Cat wriggled her way into my lap, padded up my chest and gingerly placed a paw on my chin. In an instant, my grousing about Congressional corruption fell away as I buried my fingers in her fur. Soon we were both purring with pleasure.

Day by day, in the midst of everyday-ness, joy can be hard to remember, much less muster. We have minds designed for survival. We live in bodies that break, families that harm, a world full of hurt. But joy isn't dependent on circumstances or good fortune. We don't need to be freshly in love or healthy or a four-year-old at the beach to access it. Joy isn't doled out to some more than others. Even in a rainstorm, the sun is shining somewhere.

Slow down. Get quiet. Look at life through a lens of wonder and you just may notice that joy—like waves at the water's edge—is always there, arriving with a wink.

—∿—

We cannot cure the world of sorrows,
but we can choose to live in joy.

—JOSEPH CAMPBELL

Strength

A reservoir of power
from which to draw in times of trouble

TWIG THIN WITH BUCK TEETH sheathed in braces, I spent my adolescence with my head down, getting stoned and drinking beer when I enjoyed neither. There are leaders and there are followers and in junior high, I was the caboose—tagging along, mute and powerless. Mary and I had been good friends in elementary school. We skated on Longfellow Pond in the winter and ran through sprinklers in the summer. But in the social lawlessness of seventh grade, our paths diverged. She became a target—bullied and set to drift alone in middle school purgatory—and I did nothing. I stood by, a silent witness, averting my eyes and staring at my shoes as she was humiliated. For the balance of junior and senior high, Mary was a shadow on the fringes until graduation when she disappeared into the streets, ambushed by heroin. A decade later, she was dead, an early victim of AIDS.

The thought of my betrayal haunts me. What would have happened had I come to her defense? Could I have saved her? Probably not. I imagine her demons ran deeper than my disloyalty but my cowardice is a shame I carry—a waving flag to my weakness, the price of preserving my own well-being at the expense of someone else's.

Life can be harsh. We lose jobs, watch people die, endure the thorny bramble of being twelve. After we staunch the bleeding, we reach for something to count on, to trust. Not everyone believes in God but whether they know it or not, everyone has a place inside—a voice, a touchstone, a moral compass—they can turn to for solace and counsel. *This* is where strength lives, where we know right from wrong, where we hear the whisper that tells us to stand up and fight back. The problem is we often don't, can't, won't listen.

For thirty years, I was too busy tracking the outside world to know I had an inner one worth exploring. Befriending that inner strength took decades. I had to learn to get quiet, sit still, tune out other people's voices so I could hear my own. What I know now is that real strength comes from knowing the contours of our inner landscape. Running through us is a core of strength, as strong and unbending as rebar—a rod of steel we can turn to when the winds of circumstance blow hard and a friend cries out for help.

—⁂—

What lies behind you and what lies in front of you,
pales in comparison to what lies inside of you.

—Ralph Waldo Emerson

Simplicity

Freedom from complexity

I HAVE THREE JOBS, TWO cats, a family, a wife, a body, a house, a city, a country, a world—all of which I worry about every day. There's global warming, sexual harassment, homelessness, AR-15s, teeth to floss, hair to dry, a refrigerator to stock, clients to assuage, apps to update, campaigns to wage, ad infinitum. It's all too much, a relentless parade of to-dos and responsibilities sprinkled with breaking news that's breaking me. Modern life is complicated.

But then there's the beach at daybreak. It's simple there. I know what I'll find. Sky, sand and sea, none of which need anything from me. I like it that way. My bank balance or the curl of my hair is as irrelevant to the Pacific Ocean as is the latest political scandal or, for that matter, rising sea levels. The waves don't care what they crash against. At the ocean, what matters to me is the strand of pelicans gliding at the water's surface, the nickel grey cloud passing overhead, the dawning notion that I get to live here.

At the beach, the choke hold of time loosens. Future and past recede as the present steps forward. There among the rhythms, cycles and expanse I am made right-sized, stripped of any illusion that I'm important or powerful enough to control the chaos. I stop grappling and stand on the earth. Like the sand underfoot, my mind gives way and I just breathe—simple and spare.

—❧—

Simple in actions and in thoughts,
you return to the source of being.

—Lao Tzu

Listening

Honoring the moment with attention

I AM, AMONG OTHER THINGS, a career advisor at a public agency. Recently I met with a client who had no job, no money, no family, no friends, no hope. Her debilitating back pain, outdated skills and failing eyesight made her job prospects bleak. The threat of homelessness cast a heavy shadow. As she recounted her story, my mind flew into its typical job-search-fix-it mode, which was quickly overrun by a feeling of inadequacy followed by an impulse to flee. Her problems were too deep, too real, too much responsibility. I wasn't skilled enough or paid enough for this pressure. *I hate my job.* But then, through my internal bedlam, I heard her voice crack. I blinked and saw tears streaming down her face, no match for the thin government-issue tissues I slid across my desk. This woman was terrified. Maybe listening was a good enough place to start. That much I could do.

I gave her my undivided attention, nodding in sympathy, wincing at her string of bad luck. For ten minutes,

I became a vessel into which she poured her sorry tale. When her story was finally spent, she let out a laden breath and we sat in silence for a moment, the air between us resonant. When her eyes lifted from her lap, I saw they were clearer. Her terror had, for the moment, receded.

For the balance of our session, we worked on solutions and when she left my office she was armed with a long list of social service agencies that would, at least temporarily, keep homelessness and hunger at bay. Providing referrals and resume tips was my job but so was listening. By offering a place to lay her burdens down, I had freed her hands to take up something new.

Minds are noisy. They rattle on incessantly, analyzing, judging, replaying the past, planning for the future. To stop the endless prattling is, for most us, hard. But when we're able to turn down the cerebral noise and shift our focus outward, we become available to what is presenting itself. To listen is to honor something above the mutterings of our own mind. To listen well is to be present to the moment—to savor, bitter or sweet.

—m—

Courage is what it takes to stand up and speak. Courage is also what it takes to sit down and listen.

—WINSTON CHURCHILL

Silence

A state of quietude, a place of presence.

WHERE THERE IS SILENCE, THERE can also be
screaming. When I first started meditating
in college, my mind was a swarming nest of
buzzing wasps, jumping from worry to worry: unrequited
love, unfinished homework, absent friends, dozing feet,
the urge for a cigarette. Sitting cross-legged on the floor
of my dorm, thoughts blared but I stuck with it, listening
to mania, waiting for some peace. Then, one afternoon, it
happened. In between two thoughts, at the bottom of an
exhale, my mind went momentarily quiet and the silence
was vast and empty and potent—a prairie of the mind. A
broad, peaceful meadow into which I could wander. No
judgment, no boundaries, no noise.

There's a reason monks and the spiritually aspirant
take refuge in monasteries perched on promontories high
above the sea. Cloistered from media frenzy, shopping
malls and the tyranny of conversation, seekers hope to
hear the divine. Thoughts of the past and future are set

aside in lieu of the hushed, unsullied present. To live every moment in that pure, holy silence is near impossible—yet they try, because in that deep well is peace and communion with something they sense is sacred.

Life can be noisy. As I write this I hear the clicking of my keyboard, the hum of my hot tub, wind in the trees, the rattle of buttons and zippers as they tumble in the dryer's metal drum. Silence doesn't come easily. We are talkers, doers, producers, consumers. Businesses bombard our senses with enticing messages that our hungry minds absorb. It takes conscious, deliberate effort to quiet the external storm, not to mention the internal one.

But silence is patient—a weathered bench at the edge of an open field, waiting for us to show up and sit down. To experience this silence—even if it's only a moment between breaths—is to catch a glimpse of heaven. To dwell in silence is to commune with yourself and actually enjoy the company.

—❧—

Silence is not the absence
of something, it is the
presence of everything.

— JOHN GROSSMAN

Reconciliation

Building bridges across differences

S OMETIMES IT FEELS IMPOSSIBLE TO not take sides. In a media-infused, free-market society there are mighty forces intent on creating division. There is profit and power to be gained from separation. As inequity and dissension mount, chasms grow deeper. We hole up with our own kind, maligning the enemy from the safety of our enclaves.

What would happen if our intent was to come together and connect? What would we hear from the man desperate to build a border wall or the family intent on scaling it? What would we learn from the Planned Parenthood patient or the protesters at its door? From the Israeli, the Palestinian, the Black Lives Matter marcher, the man waving a swastika lit by a torch. If we listened past our preconceptions, what truths would be revealed? If we asked the right questions, what prayer might we hear?

People are more than what they say or how they say it. Each of us has disparate parts of ourselves, oftentimes operating in contradiction. I know I do. Just as I can be kind, I can be nasty—sharp-tongued and sarcastic, dismissive and judgmental. But I know those defects to be façades I've built to keep hurt at bay. Everyone—everyone—is more than what they present to the world. To connect is to look beneath the surface where roots burrow deep.

There are seven billion of us on earth. Our skin is of different shades, we make different choices, live under different gods and governments. Each of us is a unique incarnation, unlike any other. Yet, we all come to life—and leave it—along the same path. We all eat, dance, create art and nurse dreams for our children. Reconciliation is what happens when we choose to look past what separates us to where we are, in fact, the same. There, in that realm, under that sky, is where we'll find the peace and common ground we crave—sacred and waiting.

—⚊—

We do not weave the web of life,
we are merely a strand in it.

Whatever we do to the web,
we do to ourselves.

– CHIEF SEATTLE

Appendix

313 More
Reasons for Hope

J UST IN CASE YOU THOUGHT there were only fifty-two reasons for hope, think again. Here are 313 more. Or, 365 ways of being, qualities to embody, gifts of life to enjoy.

I choose...

A
Absolution
Achievement
Acknowledgment
Action
Adeptness
Adoration
Affability
Affection
Affirmation
Agency
Alertness
Alignment
Aliveness
Altruism
Amazement
Amiability

Artistry
Ascendancy
Aspiration
Assurance
Attention
Audacity
Authenticity
Availability
Awe
Awareness
Awesomeness

B
Belief
Benevolence
Blessing
Bliss

Boldness
Bounty
Bravery
Breath
Broadmindedness
Buoyancy

C
Candor
Capacity
Care
Ceaselessness
Centeredness
Certitude
Charity
Cheerfulness
Chivalry

Circumspection
Citizenry
Civility
Comfort
Commitment
Companionship
Competence
Compliance
Composure
Concern
Confidence
Congeniality
Conscientiousness
Constancy
Contemplation
Contribution
Conviction
Cooperation
Cordiality
Courteousness
Craving
Credibility

D
Decency
Decisiveness
Dedication
Deference
Deliberation
Delicacy
Delight
Deliverance
Dependability
Depth
Desire
Detachment
Determination
Devotion
Diligence

Directness
Discernment
Discipline
Diversity
Divine order
Doing
Dominion
Dream
Duty
Dynamism

E
Eagerness
Earnestness
Earth
Ecstasy
Effectiveness
Elation
Empowerment
Encouragement
Energy
Engagement
Enlightenment
Enthusiasm
Equity
Excellence
Excitement
Existence
Expansiveness
Expectancy
Expertise
Exploration
Expression
Exuberance

F
Fairness
Fascination
Fearlessness

Festivity
Fellowship
Fertility
Fire
Flexibility
Fluency
Focus
Forbearance
Friendliness
Fruitfulness
Fulfillment

G
Geniality
Genuineness
God
Graciousness
Gratification
Guidance
Gusto

H
Happiness
Harmony
Health
Heart
Heaven
Helpfulness
High-spiritedness
Honesty
Honor
Hospitality
Humaneness
Humility
Humor

I
Idealism
Illumination

Imagination
Impartiality
Incorruptibility
Independence
Industriousness
Infinity
Influence
Ingenuity
Innocence
Inquiry
Insight
Inspiration
Insurgency
Integration
Integrity
Intelligence
Intent
Intensity
Intimacy
Intuition
Involvement

J
Journey
Joviality
Jubilance
Justice

K
Knowledge
Kinship

L
Laughter
Leniency
Liberation
Light-hearted
Liveliness
Longing

Loyalty
Luminosity

M
Magnetism
Magnificence
Mastery
Maturity
Meaningfulness
Mercy
Moderation
Modesty
Morality
Motion
Motivation
Movement
Music
Mysticism

N
Nature
Nourishment
Nurturance

O
Obedience
Objectivity
Optimism
Orderliness
Originality

P
Participation
Passion
Patience
Patriot
Perception
Perseverance
Persuasion

Philanthropy
Piety
Playfulness
Pleasure
Plenty
Poetry
Poise
Politeness
Positivity
Potency
Potential
Practicality
Practice
Praise
Preparation
Presence
Pride
Progressiveness
Promise
Prosperity
Protection
Purposefulness

Q
Quiet

R
Radiance
Rapture
Realism
Receptivity
Recognition
Reflection
Relaxation
Reliability
Resilience
Respect
Responsibility
Responsiveness

Restraint
Resistance
Reverence
Revolution
Righteousness
Rigor
Risk

S
Sacrifice
Satisfaction
Selflessness
Service
Simplicity
Sincerity
Sobriety
Sociability
Softheartedness
Solace
Solemnity
Solidity
Soulfulness
Sparkle
Spirit
Spontaneity
Stability
Steadfastness
Steadiness
Studiousness
Submission
Subtlety
Sufficiency
Surety
Sweetness
Symmetry
Sympathy

T
Tactfulness

Temperance
Tenacity
Thoughtfulness
Thoroughness
Timeliness
Tolerance
Tranquility
Treasure
Transformation
Triumph
Trust

U
Unconditionality
Understanding

V
Versatility
Vibrancy
Victory
Vigilance
Vigor
Virtue
Vitality

W
Warmth
Wholeheartedness
Willingness
Wisdom

Y
Yearning

Z
Zaniness
Zeal
Zest

50 Questions

For pondering

Here are some questions to inspire further thinking. Fill in the blank with the quality you are considering.

1. How might you embody _____ more today?

2. How does _____ operate, or not, in your life today?

3. What could your life look like if you chose to be _____ ?

4. The quality I feel called to today is _____ .

5. Who in your life today best exemplifies _____ ?

6. Who in history embodies _____ ?

7. What is the upside of _____ ?

8. What is the downside of _____ ?

9. What scares you most about _____ ?

10. What gifts would _____ bring to your life?

11. Where in your life is _____ easy?

12. Where in your life is _____ hard?

13. What is the opposite of _____ ?

14. What assumptions do you make about _____?
Are they true?'

15. What do you believe is true about _____ ?

16. What do you have wrong about _____ ?

17. What would you need to do to experience
_____ more fully?

18. Why is _____ important?

19. How can _____ make the world a better place?

20. What action can you take to strengthen your capacity
to be _____ ?

21. What would you tell your children about
_____?

22. When was the last time you experienced
_____ ?

23. How does it feel when you create or share _____
with others?

24. What do you like most about _____ ?

25. Where in your body does _____ dwell?

26. What is it about _____ that you believe is
impossible? Is it really?

27. What would it look like if you turned up the volume on
_____ ?

28. What are you avoiding about _____? Why?

29. What about _____ is confusing?

30. What excites you about _____ ?

31. What has _____ added to your life?

32. What have you rejected about _____ that seems determined to claim you?

33. What beliefs do you have about _____?

34. What do you know for sure about _____?

35. Which quality has screamed for your attention *for years*?

36. How did you experience _____ as a child? What were the repercussions?

37. What wound can be healed with _____ ?

38. Are there circumstances that make being _____ easier?

39. What would you need to change to experience _____ more fully?

40. Where do think _____ comes from?

41. How would your family benefit from _____?

42. How would your country benefit from _____?

43. How would your community benefit from more _____?

44. How would our world benefit from more _____ ?

45. What about _____ have you forgotten?

46. Why does _____ matter?

47. What happens when there is no _____ in the world? In your life?

48. What would you need to let go of to experience more _____ ?

49. What did your parents teach you, or not, about _____ ?

50. What about _____ brings you joy?

Reflections

in Alphabetical Order

About the Author

AS A CAREER COUNSELOR AT a public agency for fifteen years, Cathy Krizik has sat with thousands of people navigating the troubled waters of unemployment, earning her the title of "Minister of Hope." She grew up in an alcoholic home and spent decades lost in a fog before stumbled into Al Anon where her awakening began. Rooted in atheism, Cathy learned to meditate, studied metaphysics and, over time, crafted a daily spiritual practice that transformed her life. In spite of multiple run-ins with a surgeon's scalpel, career overhauls, a broken heart or two and the deluge of bad news that floods us all every day, she remains an unapologetic believer in the blessing of life.

Cathy holds a B.A. in art history and a M.A. in counseling. When she's not working with job seekers, she's a magazine art director and graphic designer for organizations committed to diversity, inclusion and social justice. Her writing has appeared in *The Utne Reader, North Dakota Quarterly, Evening Street Revie*w, and *Rubbertop Review*, among others. An essay about hospice and the right to die earned her a Pushcart Prize nomination. Cathy lives with her wife and two cats in Santa Cruz, CA, where the redwoods meet the sea.

To stay connected go to:
cathykrizik.com

DEDICATED TO:

the lonely and disenfranchised
the stuck and confused
the scared and imprisoned
the angry and intolerant
the lost and grasping
the small and flailing
our planet and her people

29836134R00095

Made in the USA
San Bernardino, CA
19 March 2019